The Promise of the Land

A Passover Haggadah

Rabbi Ellen Bernstein • Artwork by Galia Goodman

BEHRMAN HOUSE

www.behrmanhouse.com

Editorial consultants:

Rabbi Jonathan Brumberg-Kraus, Professor of Religion and Coordinator of Jewish Studies at Wheaton College (MA); author, *Gastronomic Judaism as Culinary Midrash* (Lexington, 2018)

Rabbi William Cutter, PhD, Professor Emeritus of Hebrew Literature and Human Relations, HUC-JIR

Ellen Rank, Senior Education Consultant, The Jewish Education Project

Rabbi Daniel Swartz, Executive Director of the Coalition on the Environment and Jewish Life (COEJL) and spiritual leader of Temple Hesed, Scranton, PA

Editor: Dena Neusner
Designer: Zahava Bogner

Published by Behrman House, Inc.
Millburn, New Jersey 07041
www.behrmanhouse.com

ISBN 978-0-87441-979-5
Printed in the United States of America

Library of Congress Cataloging-in-Publication Data
    Names: Bernstein, Ellen, 1953- author. | Goodman, Galia, illustrator.
Title: The promise of the land : a Passover Haggadah / by Rabbi Ellen
    Bernstein ; artwork by Galia Goodman.
Description: Millburn, New Jersey : Behrman House, [2020] | "This haggadah
    explores themes of nature and the land within the Passover seder, to help
    participants develop an ecological understanding of and connection with
    Jewish tradition. It includes core Passover texts, with sidebars and
    additional features that uncover the connections between the seder and the
    land"--Provided by publisher. | Includes bibliographical references. |
    Selections from the Haggadah in Hebrew with English translation and
    romanized Hebrew; commentary in English.
Identifiers: LCCN 2019020800 | ISBN 9780874419795
Subjects: LCSH: Haggadah--Adaptations. | Haggadot--Texts. |
    Seder--Liturgy--Texts. | Judaism--Liturgy--Texts. | Nature--Religious
    aspects--Judaism.
Classification: LCC BM674.795 .B47 2020 | DDC 296.4/5371--dc23 LC record available at
https://lccn.loc.gov/2019020800

Artist's Note: My artwork is a kaleidoscope of materials, colors, and textures that express how I see the world. I use paper, paints, ink, scraps of materials, my own drawings and sketches, and natural materials such as leaves, wood chips, and feathers, collaged into colorful shapes and geometric forms.

This book was printed on paper certified by the Forest Stewardship Council, a not-for-profit organization that promotes environmentally, socially, and economically responsible management of the world's forests.

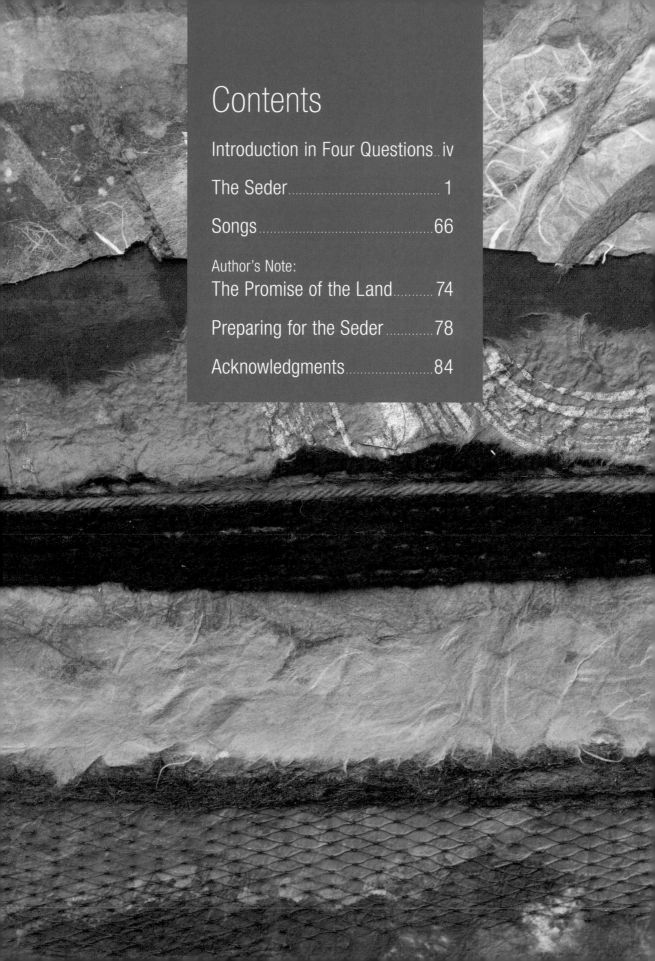

Contents

Introduction in Four Questions

WHY A NEW HAGGADAH FOR PASSOVER?

On Passover we celebrate the Jewish people's journey from slavery to freedom and the coming of spring. We tell the story year after year. Yet, for every story about peoplehood, there is a backstory about land and the natural world. Our biblical holidays commemorate the harvest and the land, the very soil out of which Judaism grew. The haggadah, the Jewish people's origin story, is necessarily embedded in an earthy reality.

Today, we are deeply aware that our well-being and our freedom depend on the earth's well-being. If the earth and its systems are compromised, our freedom is compromised; life is compromised. This haggadah seeks to enlarge our focus. It seeks to reveal the seder's ecological dimensions and awaken its quiescent environmental meaning.

HOW IS THIS HAGGADAH DIFFERENT FROM OTHER *HAGGADOT*?

The haggadah you have in your hands is traditional in some respects and modern in others. It follows the ancient instructions for Passover to read the entire passage that begins "My father was a wandering Aramean," which recaps Judaism's origin story. Curiously, the very first haggadah, which was composed hundreds of years after the instructions for the seder were written down, never actually cited the *whole* passage. The early rabbis dropped the last two verses, about land. Yet these deleted verses transmit a deep ecological message. This haggadah retrieves these two verses, re-establishing them at the heart of the seder, restoring the environmental significance of Judaism's central story.

For more on this subject, see the Author's Note on page 74.

WHAT IS "THE PROMISE OF THE LAND"?

"The promise of the land" refers to the primary blessing that God gives all the ancestors in the Bible: *eretz*, or land. That the Hebrew word *eretz* means not just "land" but also "earth" conveys a profound ecological sense. The land or earth is the home of the swimming creatures, the flying creatures, the walking, climbing, crawling, hopping, and sprinting creatures, and us. The land, the earth, is our habitat, and we are its inhabitants. Land or earth is the most precious blessing a people can receive—it is the source of sustenance; it is the promise of life, the promise of freedom.

Unfortunately, many people regard land as lifeless and inert—real estate to be bought and sold or territory to be acquired and owned. And many Jews conflate "land" with the land of Israel only. If people view land this way, the whole subject of land invariably turns economic or political, and the deeper ecological meaning of land is lost. When we approach the seder with a broader appreciation of land—its spiritual, aesthetic, and ecological value—the haggadah reveals its deep environmental meaning.

WHO IS THIS HAGGADAH FOR?

This haggadah is intended for those who are curious and want to dig deep. It understands the Passover story in universal and mythic terms. It is written for people with little or no background in Judaism as well as those with strong backgrounds—be they religious, spiritual, or secular. It aspires to reconnect participants to the beauty of the holiday and the world, while exploring essential questions about who we are and where we come from.

How to Use This Haggadah

NAVIGATING THE SEDER

The seder tells the story of the Jewish people; it is a jumping-off point for a conversation about the meaning of slavery and freedom. You can use this haggadah to create the kind of celebration you want. Feel free to linger on any page to explore a particular idea or question in more depth.

To help you navigate through the seder, the text is color-coded. The green typeface signifies traditional seder text, while the black signifies context and commentary from an ecological perspective. The sidebars offer additional insights and discussion starters to enrich the conversation. One way to use the haggadah is to simply take turns reading aloud the main text (in black) and recite the traditional text (in green) together. You might invite guests to choose a sidebar that speaks to them and share it with the group. Then let the conversation unfold.

The artwork evokes aspects of the Passover story and offers additional opportunities for reflection and discussion. Many people will respond more to a visual midrash (story) than to text. Invite their interpretations of the art.

CELEBRATING TOGETHER FROM AFAR? VISIT BEHRMANHOUSE.COM/SEDER FOR TIPS

TALKING ABOUT GOD

God is a central character in the Passover story, so it can be worthwhile to consider how to help guests who may be uncomfortable with God language feel at home at the seder. Judaism offers many understandings and metaphors for God. God is known as the breath of life or *ruach Elohim*, rock, eagle, nursing mother, and bringer of rain. God's Hebrew name—spelled *yud, hay, vav, hay*—can be translated as "One who causes being." God is the force, the mystery of the universe beyond our control. In ecological terms, God is the Oneness that connects all things.

The Jewish people are called Israel, or Yisrael, which means "one who wrestles with God." To be Jewish means to wrestle with the meaning of God—not necessarily to "believe" in God. This haggadah integrates these understandings and invites readers to consider God as the ancient rabbis often did, as Hamakom or the Place, the One that connects and sustains all places and the creatures that inhabit them.

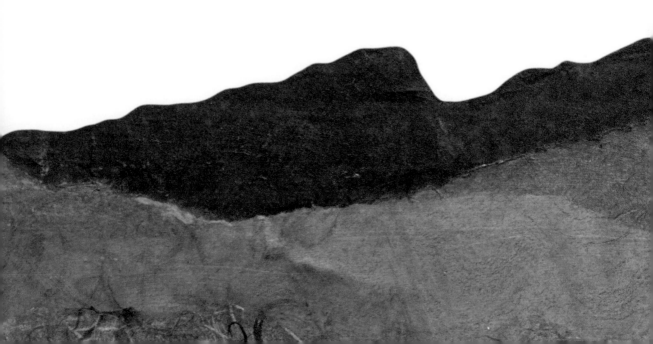

The Search for Leaven (*Chameitz*)

Passover comes at the cusp of spring, bidding us to throw off the shackles of winter and make way for a rush of fresh air. Just as we clean our homes of dirt, at Passover we also clean them of leaven (*chameitz*)—any products made of wheat, spelt, barley, oats, and rye, which rise when exposed to water. The deep cleaning of our homes points us inward toward a deep cleaning of ourselves. We seek to rid ourselves of anything that puffs us up and leads us to believe we are more important than we are. Passover is a ritual of humility.

Just before Passover, you may decide, as is traditional, to collect anything that contains *chameitz*, such as bread and noodles, and either donate them to a food pantry or put them in a designated cabinet and seal it for Passover.

On the night before the seder—if you have young children—you may want to cap the hunt for *chameitz* with a ceremonial search for the last crumbs. Inspect the corners of the house with a candle, use a feather to sweep out any specks of *chameitz*, and then scoop them up with a spoon.

"In earlier times, emptying your home of *chameitz* would have been a statement of optimism that your needs would be provided for in the new agricultural year."
—CHARLIE MILLER

"If you keep a sourdough culture year-round, Passover is an opportunity to exercise your 'faith' bone. Get rid of your culture! Don't sell or stash it away. You can always capture more yeast from the environment. When you trust that your needs will be met, you may feel more connected to the breath of life and the world around you."
—JONATHAN DUBINSKY

RECITE THE BLESSING BEFORE SEARCHING FOR *CHAMEITZ*:

בָּרוּךְ אַתָּה, יְיָ אֱלֹהֵינוּ, מֶלֶךְ הָעוֹלָם, אֲשֶׁר קִדְּשָׁנוּ
בְּמִצְוֹתָיו וְצִוָּנוּ עַל בְּעוּר חָמֵץ.

Blessed are You, Eternal our God, Force of the universe, who makes us holy with Your *mitzvot*, by commanding us to remove all *chameitz*.	*Baruch Atah, Adonai Eloheinu, Melech ha'olam, asher kid'shanu b'mitzvotav v'tzivanu al bi'ur chameitz.*

RECITE THE FORMULA FOR DISOWNING UNSEEN *CHAMEITZ* AFTER THE SEARCH FOR *CHAMEITZ*:

All *chameitz* in my possession—which I have not seen or removed and about which I am unaware—shall be nullified and ownerless as the dust of the earth.

Consider the word "ownerless." This idea of ownerlessness is significant and will resurface in the haggadah's central midrash (story).

Jewish holidays begin in the transitional space of evening. Take a moment to walk outdoors and face east. If it's a clear night, you will see the full moon of the Hebrew month of Nisan rising. It's a wonderful way to remember that our holidays are tuned to the cycles of nature.

In many traditions, fire is a symbol of transformation. We circle our hands three times over the candles and soak in the light, opening ourselves for what's to come.

Candle-Lighting

We light candles to mark the end of a work day and the beginning of a holy day. Ordinary time gives way to sacred time, inviting us to see in a new light.

LIGHT THE CANDLES AND RECITE TOGETHER:

בָּרוּךְ אַתָּה, יְיָ אֱלֹהֵינוּ, מֶלֶךְ הָעוֹלָם, אֲשֶׁר קִדְּשָׁנוּ בְּמִצְוֹתָיו וְצִוָּנוּ לְהַדְלִיק נֵר שֶׁל (שַׁבָּת וְשֶׁל) יוֹם טוֹב.

Blessed are You, Eternal our God, Force of the universe, who makes us holy with Your *mitzvot*, by commanding us to light [the Shabbat light and] the festival light.

Baruch Atah, Adonai Eloheinu, Melech ha'olam, asher kid'shanu b'mitzvotav v'tzivanu l'hadlik ner shel [Shabbat v'shel] Yom Tov.

Whenever we do something for the first time in a year, we recite the Shehecheyanu blessing. We recite the words with intention so that this special moment doesn't slip away unnoticed.

RECITE TOGETHER:

בָּרוּךְ אַתָּה, יְיָ אֱלֹהֵינוּ, מֶלֶךְ הָעוֹלָם, שֶׁהֶחֱיָנוּ וְקִיְּמָנוּ וְהִגִּיעָנוּ לַזְּמַן הַזֶּה.

Blessed are You, Eternal our God, Force of the universe, who has given us life, sustained us, and brought us to this time.

Baruch Atah, Adonai Eloheinu, Melech ha'olam, shehecheyanu, v'kiy'manu, v'higi'anu laz'man hazeh.

The Seder

The Fifteen Steps of the Seder

קַדֵּשׁ
Kadeish
Making Holy

וּרְחַץ
Urchatz
Washing

כַּרְפַּס
Karpas
Fruit of the Soil

יַחַץ
Yachatz
Splitting

מַגִּיד
Maggid
Telling

רָחְצָה
Rochtzah
Washing

מוֹצִיא
Motzi
Bringing Forth

מַצָּה
Matzah
Matzah

מָרוֹר
Maror
Bitter Herb

כּוֹרֵךְ
Koreich
Wrapping

שֻׁלְחָן עוֹרֵךְ
Shulchan Oreich
The Set Table

צָפוּן
Tzafun
Hidden

בָּרֵךְ
Bareich
Blessing

הַלֵּל
Hallel
Praising

נִרְצָה
Nirtzah
Parting

The seder's fifteen steps are a reminder of the fifteen steps leading up to the ancient Temple in Jerusalem.

The ancient rabbis suggested that the four cups of wine correspond to a four-part process of becoming free: "I will **bring** you out from under the yoke of the Egyptians, I will **free** you from being slaves to them; I will **redeem** you with an outstretched arm, and I will **take** you as My people and I will be your God."
—EXOD. 6:6–7

In many Jewish homes, whenever the wine glass is lifted at the seder, the matzah is covered, so it won't feel dejected (since it's not receiving a blessing).

קַדֵּשׁ
Kadeish ◦ Making Holy

The first two steps of the seder—*kadeish* and *urchatz*—create a doorway through which we leave behind the busy outer world and enter a more reflective inner world. Time and space circumscribe our lives. To sanctify time, we recite the Kiddush; to prepare our bodies and our physical space, we wash our hands.

Wine inaugurates this holy day as it does all Jewish festivals. It elevates our meal, turning the act of eating into a sacred and joyful occasion. We drink wine to make time holy. As free people, our time is our own and we can spend it as we wish; slaves are deprived of this freedom.

On Passover, we drink four cups to soften our edges and dissolve any blocks to our happiness and our freedom. Our first cup signifies God's bringing us out of Egypt. (Exod. 6:6)

POUR THE FIRST CUP OF WINE OR GRAPE JUICE FOR YOUR NEIGHBOR.

[ON SHABBAT, ADD THE FOLLOWING.]

וַיְהִי עֶרֶב וַיְהִי בֹקֶר יוֹם הַשִּׁשִּׁי. וַיְכֻלּוּ הַשָּׁמַיִם וְהָאָרֶץ וְכָל צְבָאָם.
וַיְכַל אֱלֹהִים בַּיּוֹם הַשְּׁבִיעִי מְלַאכְתּוֹ אֲשֶׁר עָשָׂה. וַיִּשְׁבֹּת בַּיּוֹם הַשְּׁבִיעִי
מִכָּל מְלַאכְתּוֹ אֲשֶׁר עָשָׂה. וַיְבָרֶךְ אֱלֹהִים אֶת יוֹם הַשְּׁבִיעִי וַיְקַדֵּשׁ אֹתוֹ.
כִּי בוֹ שָׁבַת מִכָּל מְלַאכְתּוֹ אֲשֶׁר בָּרָא אֱלֹהִים לַעֲשׂוֹת.

There was evening, there was morning, a sixth day.
The heavens and earth and all their inhabitants were complete.
God completed by the seventh day all the work that God had done.
And God ceased on the seventh day from all the work that God had done. And God blessed the seventh day and made it holy, because on it, God ceased from all the work that God created to make.
(Gen. 1:31–2:3)

STAND AND RECITE THE KIDDUSH TOGETHER.

בָּרוּךְ אַתָּה, יְיָ אֱלֹהֵינוּ, מֶלֶךְ הָעוֹלָם, בּוֹרֵא פְּרִי הַגָּפֶן.

Blessed are You, Eternal our God, Force of the universe, Creator of the fruit of the vine.

Baruch Atah, Adonai Eloheinu, Melech ha'olam, borei p'ri hagafen.

Whatever God might mean to us, God is associated with a force larger than ourselves. God brought us out of Egypt; we didn't escape the place of slavery entirely on our own.

Even before the rabbis solidified the practice of Kiddush, the psalmist compared the Israelites to a grapevine:

"You pulled a grapevine out from Egypt. . . .

You cleared a place for it, and it rooted; it rooted and filled the land.

The mountains were covered by its shade, mighty cedars by its boughs.

It sent its branches out to the sea, its shoots to the river."

—PSALM 80, selected verses

RECLINE TO THE LEFT TO DRINK THE WINE.

בָּרוּךְ אַתָּה, יְיָ אֱלֹהֵינוּ, מֶלֶךְ הָעוֹלָם, אֲשֶׁר בָּחַר בָּנוּ מִכָּל עָם,
וְרוֹמְמָנוּ מִכָּל לָשׁוֹן וְקִדְּשָׁנוּ בְּמִצְוֹתָיו. וַתִּתֶּן לָנוּ יְיָ אֱלֹהֵינוּ
בְּאַהֲבָה (בְּשַׁבָּת: שַׁבָּתוֹת לִמְנוּחָה וּ)מוֹעֲדִים לְשִׂמְחָה, חַגִּים וּזְמַנִּים
לְשָׂשׂוֹן אֶת יוֹם (הַשַּׁבָּת הַזֶּה וְאֶת יוֹם) חַג הַמַּצּוֹת הַזֶּה, זְמַן חֵרוּתֵנוּ
(בְּאַהֲבָה) מִקְרָא קֹדֶשׁ, זֵכֶר לִיצִיאַת מִצְרָיִם. כִּי בָנוּ בָחַרְתָּ
וְאוֹתָנוּ קִדַּשְׁתָּ מִכָּל הָעַמִּים, (וְשַׁבָּת) וּמוֹעֲדֵי קָדְשֶׁךָ
(בְּאַהֲבָה וּבְרָצוֹן) בְּשִׂמְחָה וּבְשָׂשׂוֹן הִנְחַלְתָּנוּ. בָּרוּךְ אַתָּה יְיָ,
מְקַדֵּשׁ (הַשַּׁבָּת וְ)יִשְׂרָאֵל וְהַזְמַנִּים.

Blessed are You, Eternal our God,

Force of the universe,

who has chosen us

by making us holy

through Your *mitzvot*.

You have given us in love

[Shabbat for rest,]

festivals for delight,

holy days and seasons for joy,

[this Shabbat day and] this festival of

matzot, the time of our freedom, a holy gathering in

memory of the Exodus from Egypt. You have given us

[Your holy Shabbat in love and] Your holy days for delight

and gladness. Blessed are You, God, who makes holy

[the Shabbat and] the people Israel and the festivals.

In ancient times, reclining while eating was a symbol of luxury. And reclining to the left would leave the right hand free for eating.

Some *haggadot* link the four cups to the four elements: earth, water, air, and fire. This first cup is dedicated to earth, our physical home. It recalls mountains, valleys, and diverse landscapes, reminding us of the preciousness of soil. Earth is our refuge, our habitat, and the source of our sustenance.

וּרְחַץ
Urchatz ∘ Washing

CONTINUE IN A SPIRIT OF SHARING. PASS A PITCHER OF WATER, A BOWL, AND A TOWEL; AND POUR WATER TO WASH YOUR NEIGHBOR'S HANDS.

Usually, when we are about to eat a meal, we wash our hands and recite a blessing as we wash. But here, since we will wait until after our story to eat the meal, we don't say a blessing. Now we simply wash, so we can enter the seder with clean hands and a pure heart.

Look! The winter is past,
The rain is over and gone.
The scarlet blossoms have appeared in the land,
The time of the songbird has come,
The voice of the turtledove is heard in our land.
The fig tree reddens with new fruit,
The grape blossoms breathe perfume.
(Song of Songs 2:11–13)

כַּרְפַּס
Karpas ◦ Fruit of the Soil

Karpas refers to all the green vegetables—the parsley, arugula, or other greens on the table—that sprout from the soil. It symbolizes the vibrant, verdant energy of spring, of life's urge to break through the dry earth. It reminds us that the freedom to just be, to express one's inner nature, is the most essential freedom.

The salt water—into which we'll be dipping the *karpas*—represents our sweat and tears as slaves, as well as the sea out of which we and all of our creaturely ancestors evolved.

Our tradition has special blessings for grains, vegetables, and fruits—our most basic and earthy foods. Plants sustain people and animals alike. Like plants, we are born of the earth. The Hebrew language teaches this: the only difference between human (*adam*) and earth (*adamah*) in Hebrew is the letter *hay*.

As we say the words *borei p'ri ha'adamah*, we express our gratitude for the earth, *adamah*.

DIP A GREEN VEGETABLE INTO SALT WATER AND RECITE TOGETHER:

בָּרוּךְ אַתָּה, יְיָ אֱלֹהֵינוּ, מֶלֶךְ הָעוֹלָם, בּוֹרֵא פְּרִי הָאֲדָמָה.

Blessed are You, Eternal our God, Force of the universe, Creator of the fruit of the earth.

Baruch Atah, Adonai Eloheinu, Melech ha'olam, borei p'ri ha'adamah.

"This *karpas*—this green burst of life—is paired with a pool of salty tears. While salt is a contracting element, the leafy growth is an expansive element. Together they recall the balance of nature."
—RABBA KAYA STERN-KAUFMAN

Some say the word *karpas* comes from the Persian word *karaf*, meaning "parsley"; others say it is from the Greek *karpos*, meaning "fruit of the soil." Foreign words in our lexicon remind us that Jewish tradition has never been an island. Our Jewish culture—like all living, growing things—co-evolved with the cultures of which it was a part.

The letter *hay* is light and wispy; it sounds like air, reminding us of the wind, God's breath.

Years ago, in eastern Europe, potatoes took the place of leafy greens, since they were the only vegetable available for Passover so early in the spring; today many still enjoy potatoes for *karpas*.

Talk about it: When eating plant foods, we are required to recite a special blessing, but no such blessing is required for meat. Why do you think this is so?

Some follow a Yemenite ritual of marching around the room, carrying an imaginary bundle of *matzot*, enacting the Exodus. The leader asks the guests, "Where are you coming from, and where are you headed?" Guests respond, "I'm coming from Egypt, and I'm headed to Jerusalem." Feel free to improvise!

The game of "hide the matzah" is not just child's play. It is emblematic of the central story of the evening—retrieving that which has been broken.

יַחַץ
Yachatz ∘ Splitting

On Passover the three pieces of matzah symbolize the two loaves of bread on the Shabbat table, commemorating Shabbat's double portion of manna, plus an additional matzah that we break to remember our slavery and initiate the telling of our story.

Matzah is the central symbol of Passover; Passover is even called *chag hamatzot*, the holiday of matzah.

Matzah is the simplest of all foods—wheat and water, humble pie. It is parched, dry, and unassuming like the desert. When we consider matzah relative to bread, one of its meanings becomes clear. Bread is the puffed-up version of wheat, far removed from the flour and the earth from which it comes. In the context of Passover, bread symbolizes the additives and excesses that weigh us down and enslave us. Matzah reminds us of what bread would like us to forget.

Passover is the path back to basics—the earth, the wheat, and water—and our essential selves. Passover teaches that freedom comes when we rid ourselves of the burden of too much. For now, we simply admire the matzah and reflect on it—the root food of our peoplehood.

Talk about it: If matzah teaches simplicity, what foods might we want to enjoy during Passover? If matzah suggests that we enslave ourselves to the excesses of our culture, what excesses or additives might we want to avoid during Passover?

BREAK THE MIDDLE OF THE THREE *MATZOT* INTO TWO PIECES. RETURN THE SMALLER PIECE BACK TO THE PILE, AND SET ASIDE THE LARGER PIECE FOR THE *AFIKOMAN*.

The broken matzah is symbolic of our own brokenness and the brokenness of the world. Some of us have broken with the past—we may have lost a sense of history and a connection to our ancestors. Others may feel broken or detached from our earthy home. We may have lost touch with the natural world and all that it gives us freely each day.

Talk about it: Are there ways you feel broken or disconnected? How might you help heal the brokenness?

The whole matzah represents wholeness and freedom—it is the food of liberation that the Israelites ate as they hurried out of Egypt. It helps us to retrieve lost parts of ourselves so we may become whole again.

WRAP THE *AFIKOMAN* IN A NAPKIN AND HIDE IT.

Why tell this story? The Torah charges us to tell the story for the children, so that it is transmitted from one generation to the next.
We also tell the story to remind ourselves of our past, to make meaning of our present, and to consider what slavery and freedom mean today.

מַגִּיד
Maggid ◦ Telling

The word *haggadah* derives from the Hebrew word *l'haggid*, which means "to tell." It is related to the word *maggid*, which means "story" or "telling." We tell the Passover story to remember who we are and where we came from.

REMOVE THE CLOTH COVERING THE *MATZOT* SO THEY ARE IN PLAIN VIEW DURING THE TELLING OF THE STORY. RAISE THE THREE *MATZOT*, POINT TO THE BROKEN MIDDLE PIECE, AND RECITE TOGETHER:

הָא לַחְמָא עַנְיָא דִי אֲכָלוּ אַבְהָתָנָא בְּאַרְעָא דְמִצְרָיִם.

Ha lachma anya di achalu avhatana b'ar'a d'Mitzrayim.

This is the bread of affliction
that our ancestors ate in the land of Egypt.
All who are hungry, come and eat.
All who are in need, come and enjoy the Pesach (Passover) meal.
Now we are here; next year in the Land of Israel.
Now we are slaves; next year—free people.

On one hand, matzah represents our poverty; on the other, it signifies our freedom. The ancient rabbis said that a fundamental requirement for fulfilling the Passover obligation was to tell the story of moving from degradation to freedom, and that story is told right here in the matzah.

The telling of our story begins with wide-open arms. The seder bids us to invite those who are hungry to partake of our meal. It also bids us to invite those who are hungry in spirit—lonely, lost, heartsick. We bring everybody into the circle, regardless of gender, sexuality, race, age, and religion. The freedom we aspire to depends on our sharing.

The medieval rabbi Ibn Ezra suggested that slaves were fed matzah because it takes so long to digest that it staves off hunger.

Talk about it: Can telling a story set you free? Can telling a story hinder your sense of freedom? Can language change you?

מַה נִּשְׁתַּנָּה ◦ The Four Questions

POUR (DO NOT DRINK) THE SECOND CUP.

The seder begins with four questions about the special Passover foods and table rituals.

The questions can be understood in terms of identity. Who are we, and where do we come from? Two of the questions—matzah and *maror*—suggest that we are poor and enslaved, while the other two—reclining and dipping twice—imply that we are free people, living a life of luxury.

The question "How is this night different from all other nights?" is followed by four examples of how it is different. After the question, the *maggid*, the central Jewish story, offers some answers.

The Four Questions provide a prompt for guests at the table to open up a conversation. Questioning is the mark of a free person. Don't hesitate to ask!

"An infinite question is often destroyed by finite answers."
—MADELEINE L'ENGLE

Our story begins and ends with a proclamation about the significance of food. The original Passover seder opened with three questions (not four) about the matzah, *maror*, and shank bone and ended with Rabbi Gamliel's explanation of these three symbols.

The experience of eating points us back to our food's origin, the land. Farmers and people who live close to the land can even identify the place of a food's origin by its particular taste, its *terroir*.

Our people have been eating these particular foods for two thousand years. What we eat distinguishes us and sets us apart from others.

Talk about it: What does a free person eat? What about a slave?

How do the foods you eat contribute to your identity? Do your eating habits have any effect on the world?

THE YOUNGEST CHILD RECITES THE QUESTIONS:

מַה נִּשְׁתַּנָּה הַלַּיְלָה הַזֶּה מִכָּל הַלֵּילוֹת?

Mah nishtanah halailah hazeh mikol haleilot?

How is this night different from all other nights?

שֶׁבְּכָל הַלֵּילוֹת אָנוּ אוֹכְלִין חָמֵץ וּמַצָּה.
הַלַּיְלָה הַזֶּה כֻּלּוֹ מַצָּה?

*Sheb'chol haleilot anu ochlin chameitz umatzah.
Halailah hazeh, kulo matzah?*

On all other nights, we eat *chameitz* and matzah.
Why on this night, only matzah?

שֶׁבְּכָל הַלֵּילוֹת אָנוּ אוֹכְלִין שְׁאָר יְרָקוֹת.
הַלַּיְלָה הַזֶּה מָרוֹר?

*Sheb'chol haleilot anu ochlin sh'ar y'rakot.
Halailah hazeh, maror?*

On all other nights, we eat all vegetables.
Why on this night, bitter herbs?

שֶׁבְּכָל הַלֵּילוֹת אֵין אָנוּ מַטְבִּילִין אֲפִילוּ פַּעַם אֶחָת.
הַלַּיְלָה הַזֶּה שְׁתֵּי פְעָמִים?

*Sheb'chol haleilot ein anu matbilin afilu pa'am echat.
Halailah hazeh, sh'tei f'amim?*

On all other nights, we don't even dip one time.
Why on this night, two times?

שֶׁבְּכָל הַלֵּילוֹת אָנוּ אוֹכְלִין בֵּין יוֹשְׁבִין וּבֵין מְסֻבִּין.
הַלַּיְלָה הַזֶּה כֻּלָּנוּ מְסֻבִּין?

*Sheb'chol haleilot anu ochlin bein yoshvin uvein m'subin.
Halailah hazeh, kulanu m'subin?*

On all other nights, we eat either sitting or reclining.
Why on this night, do we all recline?

Physical Slavery

The ancient rabbis had different opinions about who we are, where we come from, and how slavery has shaped our story. Samuel, a third-century Babylonian rabbi, understood slavery as physical bondage and suggested that slavery began with Pharaoh. He drew on the biblical text below, "We were slaves to Pharaoh in Egypt."

SING:

עֲבָדִים הָיִינוּ, הָיִינוּ, עַתָּה בְּנֵי-חוֹרִין, בְּנֵי-חוֹרִין.

Avadim hayinu, hayinu
Atah b'nei chorin, b'nei chorin.
Avadim hayinu, atah, atah b'nei chorin. (2x)

We were slaves, now we are free.

עֲבָדִים הָיִינוּ לְפַרְעֹה בְּמִצְרָיִם.
Avadim hayinu l'faroh b'mitzrayim.

"We were slaves to Pharaoh in Egypt, but God brought us out of there with a strong hand and an outstretched arm. God took us out from there to bring us out and give us the land God swore to our ancestors." (Deut. 6:21,23)

And if the Holy One, blessed be, had not brought our ancestors out of Egypt, then we and our children and our children's children would still be enslaved to Pharaoh in Egypt. And even if we were all wise, all intelligent, all sages, and all knowledgeable in Torah, still the mitzvah would be upon us to tell about the going out from Egypt. And the more one expands on the telling of the going out from Egypt, the better.

We began our journey as slaves in Egypt. Pharaoh owned us. He treated us like a commodity. He stripped us of power and the ability to make decisions.

Pharaoh, in our story, has no name; he is simply "pharaoh of Egypt." We all lose our identity and humanity when state slavery prevails—even Pharaoh. Individuality is subsumed to a nameless, faceless institution.

The Jewish American poet Emma Lazarus wrote, "Until we are all free, we are none of us free." She was referring to her fellow Jews—poor immigrants, arriving in America, fleeing virulent Russian anti-Semitism.

Talk about it: What do Emma Lazarus's words mean to you today?

Slavery is found wherever people have no free choice and are controlled by their exploiters. Women forced into prostitution, men forced to work at hard labor, children forced to work in sweatshops, girls forced to marry older men—all are forms of slavery. More than forty million people live in slavery worldwide today.

The seder, unlike many religious rituals, encourages us to go off script and discuss our own experience of slavery and freedom: "The more one expands on the telling of the going out of Egypt, the better."

The rabbis said the very meaning of the Hebrew word *Pesach* is the "talking mouth": *peh* means "mouth," and *sach* means "talk."

14

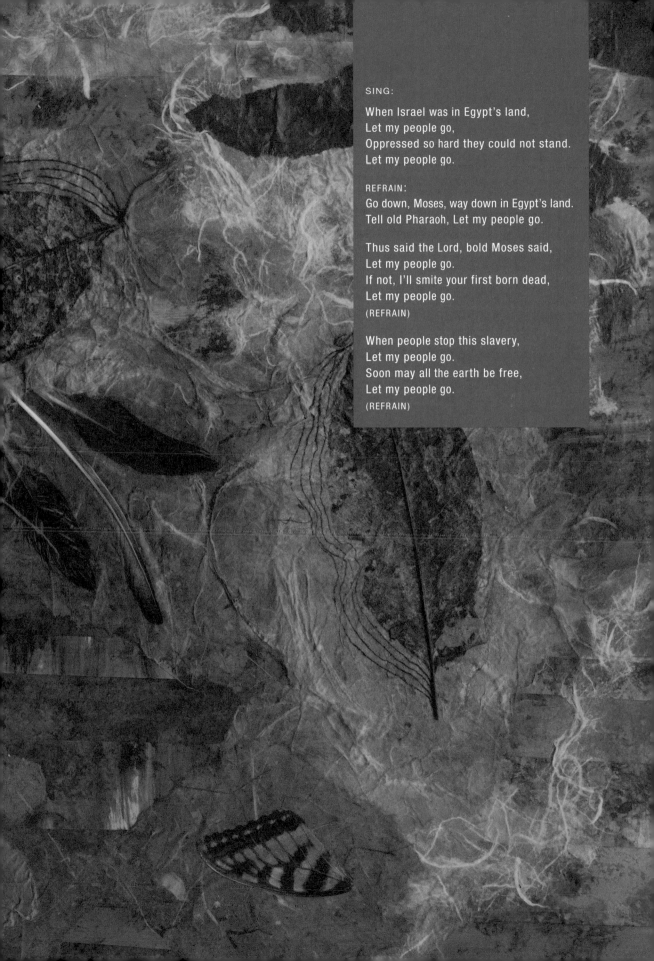

SING:

When Israel was in Egypt's land,
Let my people go,
Oppressed so hard they could not stand.
Let my people go.

REFRAIN:

Go down, Moses, way down in Egypt's land.
Tell old Pharaoh, Let my people go.

Thus said the Lord, bold Moses said,
Let my people go.
If not, I'll smite your first born dead,
Let my people go.
(REFRAIN)

When people stop this slavery,
Let my people go.
Soon may all the earth be free,
Let my people go.
(REFRAIN)

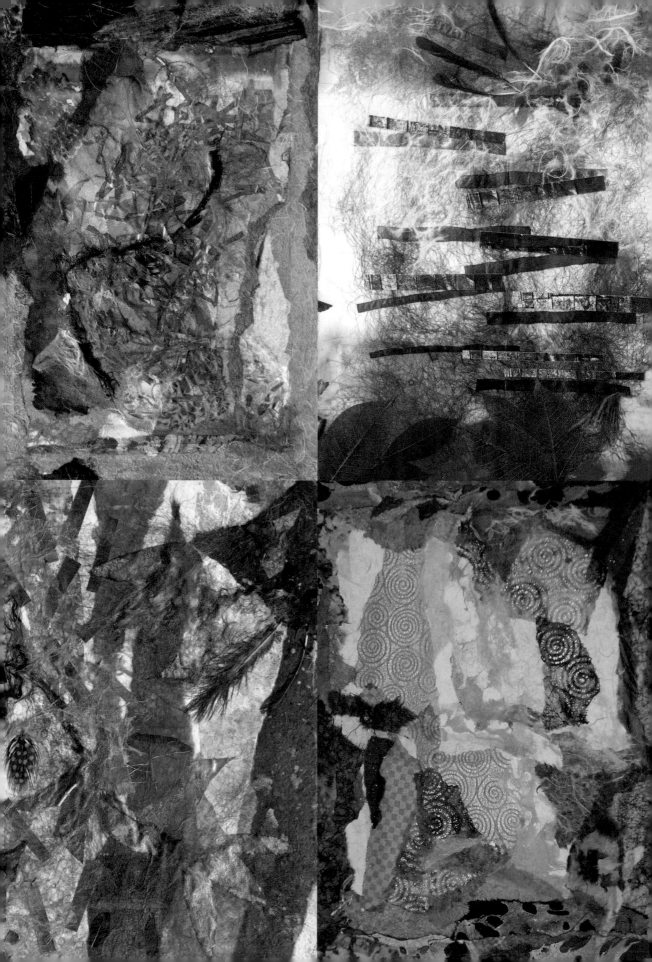

אַרְבָּעָה בָנִים · The Four Children

Earlier in the seder, the youngest child asked four questions about the foods and customs of the seder; now four children question the meaning of the service itself. In the traditional haggadah, parents offer answers by citing the Bible, but it is the questions that are significant here.

SELECT A NARRATOR AND THREE SEDER PARTICIPANTS (NOT NECESSARILY CHILDREN) TO RECITE THE QUESTIONS; YOU CAN ALSO IDENTIFY ONE WHO WILL NOT SPEAK.

מָה הָעֵדֹת וְהַחֻקִּים וְהַמִּשְׁפָּטִים, אֲשֶׁר צִוָּה יְיָ אֱלֹהֵינוּ אֶתְכֶם?

The wise child asks, "What are the testimonies, statutes, and laws which Adonai your God has commanded you?" (Deut. 6:20)

Talk about it: Which of the four children do you think would be most interested in the intricacies and mysteries of the natural world? Why?

The wise child asks a sophisticated question. She wants to discern the distinction between symbols, rules, and laws. She's interested in details. She exhibits a vibrant curiosity, and may come across as scholarly.

מָה הָעֲבֹדָה הַזֹּאת לָכֶם?

The rebellious child asks, "What does this 'service' mean to you?" (Exod. 12:26)

The word for "service" in Hebrew is *avodah*. *Avodah* means both service in terms of worship and service in terms of physical labor. *Avodah* carries both spiritual and physical meaning.

This child emphasizes the words "to you," distancing himself from the community. While it may be tempting to pigeonhole this child as the "bad boy," perhaps he simply prefers to perform his "service" outdoors chopping wood or tracing the stars in the night sky, rather than indoors in a religious ritual.

מַה זֹּאת?

The simple child asks, "What is this?" (Exod. 13:14)

The simple child asks an elementary question. Maybe she agrees with her older sibling (the rebel), whom she admires. She doesn't understand what all the fuss is about.

?

The child who doesn't know how to ask doesn't formulate a question. But this does not mean that the child is unintelligent. They may simply prefer to watch and listen or to communicate wordlessly. Their silence may be an invitation to their tablemates to pay attention to the nonverbal aspects of the seder.

Talk about it:

- Why do you think the haggadah models a family with four siblings whose characteristics do not appear entirely positive?

- Why do you think the haggadah chooses these four archetypes: wise, rebellious, simple, and one who is unable to ask? Are there other archetypes that you would add or substitute?

- Consider which child you are. Which topics capture your attention and inspire you to ask questions, and which cause you to tune out?

- Notice how people communicate at your table without words. What are they saying?

"The difference between a slave and a free person is not just a matter of social position. We can find an enlightened slave whose spirit is free, and a free man with the mentality of a slave. Real freedom is that uplifted spirit that inspires the individual . . . to remain true to their inner essence. . . . A person with a slave mentality lives life according to other people's measure of value."
—RAV KOOK

Spiritual Slavery

The third-century Babylonian rabbi known as Rav reminds us that our slavery began long before Pharaoh even lived. He claimed that ever since Abraham, we have been plagued by an insidious kind of slavery: a slavery of the mind and spirit.

The Torah teaches that our earliest ancestors worshipped idols; they were slaves to the popular ideas of their times.

מִתְּחִלָּה עוֹבְדֵי עֲבוֹדָה זָרָה הָיוּ אֲבוֹתֵינוּ,
וְעַכְשָׁו קֵרְבָנוּ הַמָּקוֹם לַעֲבוֹדָתוֹ.

The rabbis identified God here as Hamakom, or "the Place," meaning that God is present in every place all the time.

In the beginning, our ancestors worshipped idols.
But now Hamakom has drawn us close to God's service,
as it is said:
Joshua said to all the people, "This is what Adonai,
the God of Israel, says:
'Long ago your ancestors, including Terah the
father of Abraham and Nahor, lived beyond the Euphrates
River and worshipped other gods.
But I took your father Abraham from beyond the Euphrates
and led him throughout the whole land of Canaan and
gave him many descendants.
I gave him Isaac, and to Isaac I gave Jacob and Esau.
I assigned the hill country of Seir to Esau to inherit,
but Jacob and his family went down to Egypt.'"
(Josh. 24:2–4)

Abraham's father, Terah, worshipped clay statues. Jacob idolized the power of the birthright, stealing it from his brother. Joseph idolized the power of the court. The Torah does not refrain from pointing out the flaws of our ancestors.

We are not so different from our forebearers. We may pride ourselves on being open, free thinkers, but often we are slaves to the conventional ideas of our world, our friends and our family.

Idolatry is the most dangerous form of slavery because we can be oblivious to the idols that we worship.

Idolatry is a state of mind or heart, signified by Pharaoh in Egypt. The Hebrew word for Egypt, *Mitzrayim*, literally means "narrowness." The rabbis said that the narrow-minded, hard-hearted Pharaoh lives on inside of us all. On Passover, it is upon us to also confront the Pharaoh within.

"Their land is full of silver and gold, there is no limit to their treasure. Their land is full of horses, there is no limit to their chariots. And so their land is full of idols: they bow down to the work of their hands, to what their own fingers have made."—ISAIAH 2:7–8

"Affluence, no less than slavery, can make us forget who we are and why."
—RABBI JONATHAN SACKS

Talk about it: Consider the foods you eat, the products you buy. Do you consciously purchase what you want and need? Are you influenced by others or the culture in your purchasing habits? How?

"The traditional haggadah draws a sharp distinction between oppressor and oppressed—the Egyptian overlord and the Israelite slave. While our world is plagued by such stark imbalances of power, I find myself pre-occupied with the way that our society locks us, its beneficiaries, into oppressive roles. My daily routine is sustained by the ceaseless extraction and burning of fossil fuels. When I take stock of this, I want to cry out to God, not as an enslaved Israelite, but as an Egyptian, sickened by the destructive power entangled in my hands. Going back to the land—learning to grow a large portion of my family's food with regenerative techniques, drawing sustenance from the parcel of earth where we make our home while also doing my best to restore it as habitat to birds and bees, bears and butterflies—has felt, in this regard, like liberation."

—RABBI BENJAMIN WEINER

"This passage is the beating heart of the seder, recited as pilgrims brought the first fruits of the new year to the ancient Temple. It crystallizes the moment when the people would enact their embrace of the covenant, offering back to God the bounty of the land."
—CHARLIE MILLER

"When you enter the land that Adonai your God is giving you . . . take some of every first fruit of the soil, bring it from the land that Adonai your God is giving you, put it in a basket and go to the place that bears God's name. . . . Tell the priest, 'I acknowledge this day before Adonai your God that I have come into the land that Adonai swore to our ancestors to give to us.' . . . Then recite the following before Adonai your God: . . ."—DEUT. 26:1–5

Our Origin Story: My Father Was a Wandering Aramean

According to the ancient rabbis, a primary requirement for fulfilling the Passover obligation was the recitation of the biblical passage beginning "My father was a wandering Aramean." This is the Torah's shorthand encapsulation of the Exodus, the story of who we are, where we came from, and why we are here.

אֲרַמִּי אֹבֵד אָבִי.

Arami oveid avi.

My father was a wandering Aramean.
He went down to Egypt with few numbers
and sojourned there.
And there he became a great nation,
mighty and numerous.

The Egyptians dealt harshly with us and oppressed us,
and they imposed hard labor upon us.

We cried out to Adonai, the God of our ancestors;
Adonai heard our plea and saw our plight,
our misery and our oppression.

Then Adonai took us out of Egypt with a mighty hand,
with an outstretched arm,
with awesome power, with signs and with wonders.
(Deut. 26:5–8)

Adonai brought us to this place and gave us this land, a land flowing with milk and honey.

Now, I bring the first fruits of the soil which You, Adonai, have given me. (Deut. 26:9–10)

This biblical passage is perhaps the most concise telling of the Passover story, yet the traditional haggadah omitted the last two verses of the passage. (DEUT. 26:9–10) These overlooked verses provide a deep ecological context to the story. They are reclaimed and embellished in this haggadah.

אֲרַמִּי אֹבֵד אָבִי.

"My father was a wandering Aramean."

Our ancient ancestor Jacob was known as a wandering Aramean because his mother Rebecca came from Aram. The family lived as nomads, herding sheep and cattle in the lands near Canaan.

Jacob had twelve sons and one daughter. Of all the children, Jacob loved Joseph best and gave him a stunning coat that Joseph would flaunt. Joseph was a dreamer. He dreamed that his father was the sun and his mother, the moon, and his siblings, the stars, and that they all bowed down to him.

Joseph's siblings could not endure him. One day, they threw him into a pit. Joseph was found by the Midianites and was ultimately sold to Potiphar, the captain of Pharaoh's guard in Egypt. Joseph fared well in Egypt, but after a palace intrigue with Potiphar's wife—apparently she ordered him to lie with her—he was cast into a dungeon.

Joseph's knack for deciphering dreams ultimately got him out of that pit. He interpreted Pharaoh's dreams of fat and lean cows and healthy and scorched corn as a sign of a frightening weather pattern that would befall Egypt—seven years of plenty followed by seven more of drought.

Joseph's foresight would save the empire. The Egyptians could bank the excess grain during the years of plenty to provide for the years of drought. Pharaoh rewarded Joseph, crowning him second-in-command over the entire empire.

This entire passage is presented here as a midrash, or story; it follows the rabbinic tradition of citing each phrase and then drawing out its meaning.

To see the biblical sources for the story, please refer to page 85.

By centralizing the management of the land and the food distribution system, Joseph helped strengthen Pharaoh's control over the land and its inhabitants.

וַיֵּרֶד מִצְרַיְמָה וַיָּגָר שָׁם בִּמְתֵי מְעָט.

"He went down to Egypt with few numbers
and sojourned there."

The seven years of plenty came and went. Then came the famine. It extended all the way up to Canaan, but Egypt still had bread. Joseph's brothers had to travel down to Egypt to secure provisions for the clan, and there they met Joseph.

Of course, they didn't know that it was him. Initially, Joseph toyed with them—perhaps he wanted his brothers to pay for their wickedness all those years ago. But over time, Joseph realized that the difficult episodes in his life had shaped him into the man he had become. Only then could he reveal himself to his brothers.

The weather and particularly drought and famine have always determined where and how our people lived.

Meanwhile, the land of Canaan had become a wasteland. Five more years of famine still lay ahead. The clan had to leave their home in Canaan and move to Egypt—or starve.

וַיְהִי שָׁם לְגוֹי גָּדוֹל עָצוּם וָרָב.

"And there he became a great nation,
mighty and numerous."

The Egyptian lands were rich and fertile and the harvest bountiful because the Nile River would predictably overflow its banks each year, enriching the soil.

When the family arrived in Egypt, Joseph assigned them lush and fertile grounds where they could grow their crops and pasture their sheep. They and their descendants worked hard and contributed to the Egyptian economy. They were fruitful and multiplied, and their homes were noisy with exuberant children.

Many years passed, and a new Pharaoh arose who did not know Joseph. He fancied himself a god, creator of all life. He was afraid that the Israelites would rise up and join foreign armies against him.

וַיָּרֵעוּ אֹתָנוּ הַמִּצְרִים וַיְעַנּוּנוּ וַיִּתְּנוּ עָלֵינוּ עֲבֹדָה קָשָׁה.

"The Egyptians dealt harshly with us and oppressed us, and they imposed hard labor upon us."

Pharaoh tried to crush our mushrooming clan; our people were subhuman to him. He forced us to make bricks for storage cities in which to stockpile the excess grain.

An empire could amass vast amounts of grain, and as long as there was a place to store it, the empire could become enormously rich. The richer Pharaoh grew, the greedier he grew, the more he oppressed our people.

With no one in the court to look out for our ancestors and no land to call their own, our people were outsiders, aliens. Displaced and landless, we gradually became slaves. Egypt, the most powerful empire in the world, grew rich off the work of our hands.

Still, this wasn't enough to placate Pharaoh. He ordered the killing of the Israelite newborn boys. But our tireless midwives, Shifrah and Puah, resisted. They defied Pharaoh and saved as many babies as they could. They ensured our future.

Maybe the Egyptians had heard rumors of how, generations back, Joseph had manipulated the lands and the food supply, inflicting hardship on the Egyptians, while his own family had thrived.

"First Pharaoh called on the Egyptians and Israelites to work on the construction project together for pay. Then the Egyptians withdrew, leaving just the Israelites to work. Then Pharaoh stopped paying the Israelites. Gradually, the Israelites had become slaves and the Egyptians their taskmasters. It was such an incremental process that the Israelites became habituated to the situation and did not flee. They were blind to Pharaoh's evil plan."
—RABBI JONATHAN SACKS

וַנִּצְעַק אֶל יְיָ אֱלֹהֵי אֲבֹתֵינוּ וַיִּשְׁמַע יְיָ אֶת קֹלֵנוּ
וַיַּרְא אֶת עָנְיֵנוּ וְאֶת עֲמָלֵנוּ וְאֶת לַחֲצֵנוּ.

"We cried out to Adonai, the God of our ancestors;
Adonai heard our plea and saw our affliction,
our misery and our oppression."

It seemed as if we had been slaves in Egypt for an eternity.
We were demoralized and depressed and could not imagine
being free. Then we remembered a story handed down by our
ancestors: we would suffer terribly in a foreign land for four
hundred years, but in the end, God would take us out and we
would inherit a land we could call our own. The story gave us
hope, and finally we found our voice.

With all our strength, we cried out to God, the One who created
heaven and earth. It was as if the depth of our despair coupled
with a faith in an unseen God stimulated a response. Something shifted—something we will never know or understand.

וַיּוֹצִאֵנוּ יְיָ מִמִּצְרַיִם בְּיָד חֲזָקָה וּבִזְרֹעַ נְטוּיָה וּבְמֹרָא
גָּדֹל וּבְאֹתוֹת וּבְמֹפְתִים.

"Then Adonai took us out of Egypt with a mighty hand,
with an outstretched arm, with awesome power,
with signs and with wonders."

Talk about it: Might the earth
and its creatures actually
sense our oppression?

The God our ancient ancestors worshipped, an invisible God we
could barely imagine, appeared out of nowhere, creating havoc
throughout Egypt with one frightful plague after another
—bloody water, croaking frogs, dead beasts. All of creation
seemed to be convulsing in rage at Pharaoh.

עֶשֶׂר הַמַּכּוֹת ◦ The Ten Plagues

DIP YOUR FINGER INTO THE CUP OF WINE OR GRAPE JUICE AND DROP A BIT ONTO YOUR PLATE AS EACH PLAGUE IS NAMED.

דָּם
Dam
Blood

צְפַרְדֵּעַ
Tz'fardei'a
Frogs

כִּנִּים
Kinim
Lice

עָרוֹב
Arov
Wild animals (or flies)

דֶּבֶר
Dever
Pestilence

שְׁחִין
Sh'chin
Boils

בָּרָד
Barad
Hail

אַרְבֶּה
Arbeh
Locusts

חֹשֶׁךְ
Choshech
Darkness

מַכַּת בְּכוֹרוֹת
Makat b'chorot
Striking down the firstborn

Rabbi Yehuda HaLevi, the twelfth-century Spanish poet and physician, showed that eight of the plagues issued from the three habitats:

Two from water— blood and frogs,

Two from earth—lice and wild animals,

Two from air (infections)— pestilence and boils,

Two from air-carried damages—hail and locusts.

God could have sent an army to overthrow Pharaoh. But God called on creation to convey the message. The plagues perverted the entire natural order. God had created the earth and all its creatures. Now God was undoing creation—in Pharaoh's corner of the world.

Through all this, our faith in this unseen God—the creative universal life force—began to grow. When we were finally able to imagine ourselves as a free people in a land we could call home, our collective energy seemed to well up. Maybe we even roused the east wind. It blew so hard that it split the Red Sea. The waters opened up like a birth canal, and we fled from Egypt and crossed safely to the other side.

"A disaster of biblical proportions began in coastal Peru in March 1925 when an ENSO [a climate pattern] warmed the surface of the eastern Pacific Ocean . . . bringing deluging rain to a usually arid region. Large numbers of frogs, dragonflies, crickets, and mosquitoes appeared and were followed by epidemic diseases."—JOEL EHRENKRANZ AND DEBORAH SAMPSON

Could the plagues have had some basis in natural phenomena? The first plague, *dam* (blood), can be imagined as red clay washed down from the highlands during heavy rains, reddening the Nile and fouling the water. The muddy waters would wipe out the fish. The frogs, crowded out of their habitat by the dead fish, would seek the coolness of human homes (second plague). The frogs would die indoors, providing food for lice and flies, which would multiply (third and fourth plagues) and give rise to a pestilence that could infect animals and cause boils in people (fifth and sixth plagues).

The plagues can be compared to today's ecological disasters, such as the 2017 California drought induced by hot weather and followed by forest fires, which led to catastrophic and deadly mudslides.

וַיְבִאֵנוּ אֶל הַמָּקוֹם הַזֶּה וַיִּתֶּן לָנוּ אֶת הָאָרֶץ
הַזֹּאת אֶרֶץ זָבַת חָלָב וּדְבָשׁ.

"Adonai brought us to this place and gave us this land,
a land flowing with milk and honey."

Getting out of Egypt was not the hardest part. We would spend forty years wandering in the wilderness before we could receive a land where we could set roots, grow our own food, and finally be free. It would take all that time to heal from the condition of slavery that we inherited in Egypt.

In Egypt, Pharaoh owned and exploited the land and everything in it—the fruit trees, the animals, the gold deposits, and us. In Pharaoh's ownership economy, people and creatures were commodities to be bought and sold.

If we were going to inherit a land, we would need to honor the dignity of all people, all creatures, and the land. God freed the Israelites, not just for our sake, but for the sake of the entire creation. The land and its creatures belong to God.

"Land is the basis of all independence. Land is the basis of freedom, justice, and equality."—MALCOLM X

Talk about it: Can you be free without a connection to land? How might slavery be connected to landlessness?

"According to the Talmud, a squatter who cares for a piece of land for three years assumes ownership of that land. In Philadelphia there are thousands of vacant lots. Here, community groups that save threatened gardens, and networks of gardeners quietly tapping maple trees deep in the urban forests, are liberating themselves and their communities by becoming more connected to and grounded in the places that they live. They are manifesting an ethic of ownerless stewardship of the wild, right here in the city."
—NATI PASSOW

The acquiring of a wife can be compared to the acquiring of land. (MISHNAH KIDDUSHIN) In neither case does the acquiring mean taking ownership. Rather, "to acquire" means to take on more responsibility—to more consciously care for one's spouse or the land.

"A nation that destroys its soil destroys itself."
—FRANKLIN D. ROOSEVELT

"The promised land is the land where you belong. Like a *basherte* marriage—a marriage that is 'meant to be'—it is a reciprocal relationship."
—JUDY DORNSTREICH

Farmed properly in traditional ways, the land itself is one of our best defenses against the threat of climate change. Building topsoil with humus, adding organic material, minimizing soil disturbance, avoiding chemical fertilizers and pesticides, and safeguarding the ground with perennials or cover crops will, over time, increase soil carbon.

We could not own the land, because land has a life of its own. We were to treat the land as a "commons," which everyone could share and enjoy together, just as we all share the air. We were to see ourselves as God's tenants—guests on the land.

The hardest lesson for us to learn was that the land could not be guaranteed. If we neglected the land's need for rest every seventh year, if we forgot the Sabbath, if we avoided giving to the poor or hoarded the land or its produce—our behaviors would reverberate in the land. And one day, the land might be unable to endure our indifference any longer. The land may have no recourse but to spew us out.

If we wanted to dwell freely in the land for generations, we would have to know what farmers have always known: that caring for land is a matter of life and death. It requires dedication, perseverance, and love.

The whole world was created just so people could experience the gratitude that comes from harvesting their first fruits. (commentary on GENESIS RABBAH 1:4)

"On our farm, my husband would feed the soil as lovingly and attentively as a parent feeds a child. Abundant earthworms infiltrated the soil, lightening it up and aerating it, and barn swallows would swoop for insects as the land was being tilled. The well-fed soil-child reciprocated with the best-tasting, most-nourishing food imaginable."
— JUDY DORNSTREICH

We live in reciprocity with God and the land. God gives us a land, and we bring the land's fruits back to God. Returning our fruits to God ensures that the cycle of giving is unbroken.

"Today many of us are alienated from nature and the land. We forget that everything in our 'civilized' lives—food, medicine, and even plastic—comes from the natural world. For me, gardening connects me back to the land. It nourishes my spirit as much as my body. Just being in the garden, digging and getting dirty, is food for my soul. Recent research shows that exposing our skin and bodies to the soil's many microbes can enhance our physical health. The microbes in the soil work their way into our bodies through physical touch, breathing, and eating, and inoculate our microbiomes with beneficial organisms."
—DARON JOFFE

וְעַתָּה הִנֵּה הֵבֵאתִי אֶת רֵאשִׁית פְּרִי הָאֲדָמָה
אֲשֶׁר נָתַתָּה לִּי יְיָ.

"Now, I bring the first fruits of the soil which You, Adonai, have given me."

When we finally arrived in the land, we cultivated the soil and pastured our sheep. We planted seeds and tended our crops, praying for the right amount of rain at the right time. When the vineyards bore the first grapes and the fields were lush with grain, we were ecstatic.

We hurried to Jerusalem with our finest produce—eager to return to God something of what had been given to us. Along the way, we joined parades of exuberant villagers, dressed in finery, singing and playing flutes. We were escorted by oxen-drawn wagons bearing colorful baskets of fruit. (Mishnah Bikurim 3)

In those early years on the land, we lived by the cycles of seed-time and harvest, the autumn and spring rains. We knew that the land did not belong to us; we belonged to the land.

דַּיֵּנוּ • *Dayeinu*

Passover encourages us to distinguish between "more" and "enough." More wealth, comfort, and convenience often stimulate the desire for even more wealth, comfort, and convenience.

Dayeinu (literally "it would have been enough") teaches us that when we take a moment to feel satisfied with what we already have and recognize that we are blessed with not just enough, but more than enough, we free ourselves from the illusion that we need more. Dayeinu joyfully proclaims we have enough! We are blessed to be alive, to inhabit such a beautiful and bountiful world.

SING:

אִלּוּ הוֹצִיאָנוּ מִמִּצְרַיִם, דַּיֵּנוּ.
אִלּוּ נָתַן לָנוּ אֶת הַשַּׁבָּת, דַּיֵּנוּ.
אִלּוּ נָתַן לָנוּ אֶת הַתּוֹרָה, דַּיֵּנוּ.

Ilu hotzi'anu miMitzrayim, dayeinu.
Ilu natan lanu et haShabbat, dayeinu.
Ilu natan lanu et haTorah, dayeinu.

Had God brought us out of Egypt,
and not divided the sea for us, *dayeinu*!

Had God divided the sea for us,
and not provided for us in the desert, *dayeinu*!

Had God provided for us in the desert,
and not fed us with manna, *dayeinu*!

Had God fed us with manna,
and not given us the Sabbath, *dayeinu*!

Had God given us the Sabbath,
and not drawn us close at Mount Sinai, *dayeinu*!

Had God drawn us close at Mount Sinai,
and not given us the Torah, *dayeinu*!

Had God given us the Torah,
and not given us a land, *dayeinu*!

In the Sephardic tradition people playfully whip each other with scallions during the singing of Dayeinu.

Talk about it: What constitutes enough for you? What material goods do you really need and what could you do without?

Dayeinu is a poem of radical appreciation. We undermine ourselves when we imagine that we can be happy only when any one particular desire is fulfilled. Happiness is a by-product of our capacity for gratitude for all that is.

Feel free to add your own verses to Dayeinu: what would be enough in your life and what can be done without? For example:

If we used our shopping bags and avoided plastic, *dayeinu*!

If we grew our own gardens and stopped spraying pesticides, *dayeinu*!

If we invested in sustainable businesses and disinvested in polluters, *dayeinu*!

If we . . .

Talk about it: In ancient times, people celebrated holy days by giving up to God their valuable animals. How might animal sacrifice have been meaningful to them? How might the practice of spiritual or material sacrifice apply to your life today?

פֶּסַח, מַצָּה, מָרוֹר ◦ *Pesach*, Matzah, *Maror*

Rabbi Gamliel used to say that anyone who has not explained three things during the seder—*pesach* lamb, matzah, and *maror*—has not fulfilled their duty.

POINT TO THE SHANK BONE OR BEET AND SAY:

פֶּסַח, עַל שׁוּם מָה?

This *pesach* lamb—why did we eat it in ancient times?

SAY TOGETHER:

It is the Passover offering to God because "God passed over [*pasach*] the houses of our ancestors, sparing them, when God struck the Egyptians." (Exod. 12:27)

LIFT THE MATZAH AND SAY:

מַצָּה, עַל שׁוּם מָה?

This matzah—why do we eat it?

SAY TOGETHER:

It recalls the dough of our ancestors, which did not have time to rise. "The Israelites baked unleavened cakes because they were driven from Egypt and could not delay; they had no provisions for the journey." (Exod. 12:39)

LIFT THE *MAROR* AND SAY:

מָרוֹר, עַל שׁוּם מָה?

This *maror* (bitter herbs)—why do we eat it?

SAY TOGETHER:

It reminds us that the Egyptians embittered the lives of our ancestors. "They embittered their lives with hard labor—with clay and bricks and with all kinds of field labor. In all their work, they worked them ruthlessly." (Exod. 1:14)

Today many vegetarian seders substitute a beet for a shank bone.

The Israelites affirmed their commitment to God by painting their doorposts with sheep's blood. This act of resistance was all the more provocative because the Egyptians may have worshipped sheep.

"Matzah is the bread of haste. If you aren't prepared when an opportunity comes for liberation, you must take it anyhow. If you delay, if you procrastinate . . . then you will probably lose the moment in which you might act."
—MARGE PIERCY

Many Ashkenazi Jews use horseradish for *maror*, because it's so bitter that it makes you cry, but in ancient times a bitter lettuce was used. Jews in northern Europe substituted horseradish, since the lettuce didn't leaf out in time for Passover and, over time, lettuce had become less bitter.

Also on the Seder Plate

There are other foods on the seder plate, including the *karpas*, the green vegetable that symbolizes spring, that we dipped in salt water earlier.

This *chazeret* (lettuce)—why do we eat it? This second bitter herb reminds us of the bitter lettuce that was used for *maror* in ancient times.

This *beitzah* (roasted egg)—why do we eat it? It stands for the roasted holiday sacrifice and reminds us of spring, life, birth, and renewal.

Today, many people have both horseradish (*maror*) and lettuce (*chazeret*) at the seder.

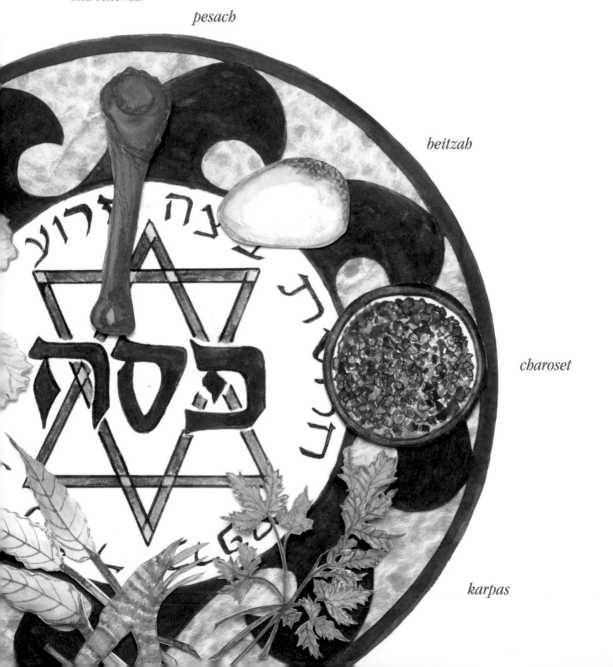

pesach

beitzah

charoset

karpas

This *charoset*—why do we eat it? It stands for the mortar used for cementing bricks for Pharaoh's storehouses.

The muddy-looking *charoset* may look like mortar but it tastes heavenly. One ancient rabbi said the *charoset*, a concoction of apples, nuts, and spices, was a remembrance of the apple tree in the Song of Songs, which is traditionally read at Passover. The Song of Songs heralds the coming of spring and celebrates the aliveness of the land and all its creatures. Seated humbly on the seder plate, the fragrant and fruity *charoset* embodies the spring and reminds us to enjoy the everyday gifts of the season that we so often take for granted.

Today, many Jews add items to the seder plate that speak to contemporary issues. An orange honors the place of women, people of color, and those of different genders and sexual orientations. It symbolizes the fruitfulness that they bring to the world. An olive is a sign of hope for peace between Israelis and Palestinians. If other foods have been placed on your seder plate, now is the time to reflect on them.

chazeret

בְּכָל דּוֹר וָדוֹר ◦ In Every Generation

בְּכָל דּוֹר וָדוֹר חַיָּב אָדָם לִרְאוֹת אֶת עַצְמוֹ
כְּאִלּוּ הוּא יָצָא מִמִּצְרָיִם.

*B'chol dor vador chayav adam lir'ot et atzmo
k'ilu hu yatza mi'Mitzrayim.*

In every generation, each of us is obligated to see ourselves as if we personally went out of Egypt, as it says, "You shall tell your child on that very day:
It's because of this that God did for me when I went out from Egypt." (Exod. 13:8)

Not only were our ancestors redeemed by the Holy One, blessed be, but we too were redeemed with them—as it says, "God took us out from there to bring us out and give us the land God swore to our ancestors." (Deut. 6:23)

"The Exodus from Egypt occurs in every human being, in every era, in every year, and in every day."
—RABBI NACHMAN OF BRATSLAV

It's not enough to recount the story; we're asked to feel the slavery in our bones and to feel the freedom that comes from living in relationship with a land.

הַלְלוּיָהּ ◦ Hallelujah

COVER THE MATZAH AND RAISE (BUT DON'T DRINK) THE SECOND CUP, AS A TOAST TO GOD, AND RECITE TOGETHER:

Therefore, we must thank, sing hallelujah, praise, exalt, elevate, beautify, bless, lift up, and laud the One who worked all these wonders for our ancestors and us. God brought us from slavery to freedom, from grief to happiness, from darkness to light, from slavery to redemption. Let's sing to the One a new song. Hallelujah!

Gratitude is the joy we feel when we realize how miraculous it is that we are even alive at all.

הַלֵל ◦ Hallel

בְּצֵאת יִשְׂרָאֵל מִמִּצְרָיִם, בֵּית יַעֲקֹב מֵעַם לֹעֵז.
הָיְתָה יְהוּדָה לְקָדְשׁוֹ, יִשְׂרָאֵל מַמְשְׁלוֹתָיו.
הַיָּם רָאָה וַיָּנֹס, הַיַּרְדֵּן יִסֹּב לְאָחוֹר.
הֶהָרִים רָקְדוּ כְאֵילִים, גְּבָעוֹת כִּבְנֵי צֹאן.
מַה לְּךָ הַיָּם כִּי תָנוּס, הַיַּרְדֵּן תִּסֹּב לְאָחוֹר.
הֶהָרִים תִּרְקְדוּ כְאֵילִים, גְּבָעוֹת כִּבְנֵי צֹאן.
מִלִּפְנֵי אָדוֹן חוּלִי אָרֶץ, מִלִּפְנֵי אֱלוֹהַ יַעֲקֹב.
הַהֹפְכִי הַצּוּר אֲגַם מָיִם, חַלָּמִישׁ לְמַעְיְנוֹ מָיִם.

When Israel came out from Egypt, when Jacob from a
people of strange speech,

Judah was God's holy one; Israel, God's domain.

The sea saw and fled; the Jordan turned backward;

The mountains danced like rams; the hills like lambs.

What was it, Sea, that you fled? Jordan, that you turned
backward?

Mountains, that you danced like rams; hills, like lambs?

Whirl, earth, in the presence of the One, in the presence
of the God of Jacob,

Who turned the rock into a pool of water, the steely rock
into a spring.

(Psalm 114)

It is traditional to sing Hallel,
six psalms of praise (PSALMS
113–118), on all pilgrimage
festivals, including Passover.
Two psalms are read before the
meal and the rest are recited
after. This haggadah includes
sections of some of the psalms
and adds a poem. Feel free to
add your own expressions of
gratitude.

i thank You God for most this amazing
day: for the leaping greenly spirits of trees
and a blue true dream of sky; and for everything
which is natural which is infinite which is yes

(i who have died am alive again today,
and this is the sun's birthday; this is the birth
day of life and of love and wings: and of the gay
great happening illimitably earth)

how should tasting touching hearing seeing
breathing any—lifted from the no
of all nothing—human merely being
doubt unimaginable You?

(now the ears of my ears awake and
now the eyes of my eyes are opened)

—e.e. cummings

כּוֹס שֵׁנִי • The Second Cup

We complete our story with a second cup of wine. This second cup also signals that the blessings we recite before a meal are about to begin.

RECITE THE BLESSING AND DRINK AT LEAST HALF THE SECOND CUP OF WINE OR JUICE, WHILE RECLINING TO THE LEFT.

RECITE TOGETHER:

בָּרוּךְ אַתָּה, יְיָ אֱלֹהֵינוּ, מֶלֶךְ הָעוֹלָם, בּוֹרֵא פְּרִי הַגָּפֶן.

Blessed are You, Eternal our God, Force of the universe, Creator of the fruit of the vine.

Baruch Atah, Adonai Eloheinu, Melech ha'olam, borei p'ri hagafen.

The second cup is associated with the biblical phrase "God will free us." (EXOD. 6:6) According to the rabbis, achieving freedom is a process. It does not happen overnight.

The second cup is dedicated to water, the circulatory system of our bodies and the circulatory system of the earth. Water reminds us of the Red Sea, the rivers, and the rain. In Hebrew, the words for "pool" and "blessing" share the same root letters. Water is the source of blessing.

רָחְצָה
Rochtzah ∘ Washing

Water is the element of transformation. According to the Hebrew blessing for hand-washing, when we wash our hands, we elevate them. Through the actions of our hands, we bring holiness to the world.

PASS AROUND A BOWL, A PITCHER OF WATER, AND A TOWEL SO PEOPLE CAN WASH THEIR HANDS. OR, IF YOU PREFER, PEOPLE CAN LIFT AND WAVE THEIR HANDS, SINCE THE HEBREW WORD FOR "WASH" HERE LITERALLY MEANS "LIFT."

RECITE TOGETHER:

בָּרוּךְ אַתָּה, יְיָ אֱלֹהֵינוּ, מֶלֶךְ הָעוֹלָם, אֲשֶׁר קִדְּשָׁנוּ בְּמִצְוֹתָיו וְצִוָּנוּ עַל נְטִילַת יָדָיִם.

Blessed are You, Eternal our God, Force of the universe, who makes us holy with Your *mitzvot*, by commanding us to wash (lift up) our hands.

Baruch Atah, Adonai Eloheinu, Melech ha'olam, asher kid'shanu b'mitzvotav v'tzivanu al n'tilat yadayim.

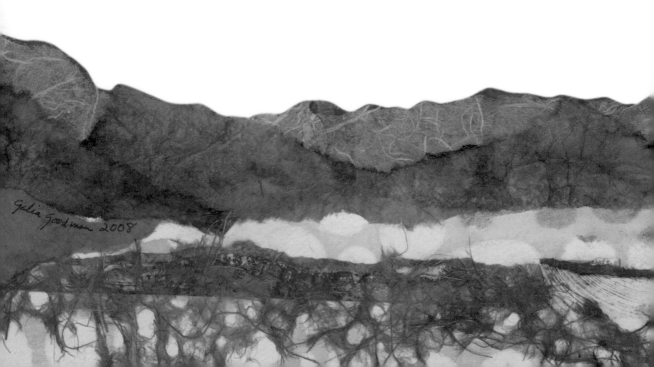

Galia Goodman 2008

מוֹצִיא
Motzi ◦ Bringing Forth

Bread is the staff of life. *Lechem* in Hebrew refers not only to bread but to all food, and we recite the blessing for bread before any meal.

We are blessed to inhabit a world in which the grasses of the field become the bread that sustains our lives.

HOLD ALL THREE *MATZOT*—THE TWO WHOLE ONES (TOP AND BOTTOM) AND THE BROKEN ONE IN THE MIDDLE—AND RECITE TOGETHER:

בָּרוּךְ אַתָּה, יְיָ אֱלֹהֵינוּ, מֶלֶךְ הָעוֹלָם,
הַמּוֹצִיא לֶחֶם מִן הָאָרֶץ.

Blessed are You, Eternal our God, Force of the universe, who brings forth bread from the earth.	*Baruch Atah, Adonai Eloheinu, Melech ha'olam, hamotzi lechem min ha'aretz.*

LOWER THE BOTTOM MATZAH (IT WILL BE USED FOR THE HILLEL SANDWICH). CONTINUE HOLDING THE UPPER AND MIDDLE *MATZOT* FOR THE NEXT BLESSING.

"How much effort did Adam the first man exert before he found bread to eat? He plowed, sowed, reaped, sheaved, threshed, winnowed, separated, ground, sifted, kneaded, and baked, and thereafter he ate. And I . . . wake up and find all these prepared for me."
—TALMUD, B'RACHOT 58A

"To be able to eat and drink is as extraordinary and miraculous as crossing the Red Sea. We do not recognize the miracle because for the moment, we live in a world of plenty and because our memory is so short."
—EMMANUEL LEVINAS

48

מַצָּה
Matzah

Matzah is the most elemental food—wheat and water. Eating matzah leads us back to the earth, to our essential selves.

We depend on other creatures, both animal and vegetable. To live, we must take from the natural world. When we do this with reverence, it is a blessing. When we do it thoughtlessly or greedily, it is a desecration.

As you eat the matzah, taste it as if for the first time. Notice the matzah's texture—its crunchiness, its lightness, its burnt edges. Remember where the matzah came from—berries of wheat, sown in the ground, watered by the rains, nurtured by the sun.

HOLD THE UPPER AND MIDDLE *MATZOT* AND RECITE TOGETHER:

בָּרוּךְ אַתָּה, יְיָ אֱלֹהֵינוּ, מֶלֶךְ הָעוֹלָם, אֲשֶׁר קִדְּשָׁנוּ
בְּמִצְוֹתָיו וְצִוָּנוּ עַל אֲכִילַת מַצָּה.

Blessed are You, Eternal our God, Force of the universe, who makes us holy with Your *mitzvot*, by commanding us to eat matzah.

Baruch Atah, Adonai Eloheinu, Melech ha'olam, asher kid'shanu b'mitzvotav v'tzivanu al achilat matzah.

BREAK THE UPPER AND MIDDLE *MATZOT* AND PASS AROUND THE PIECES.
EAT WHILE RECLINING TO THE LEFT.

49

מָרוֹר
Maror ◦ Bitter Herb

TAKE A PIECE OF ROMAINE LETTUCE AND USE IT TO SCOOP UP SOME
GRATED HORSERADISH AND *CHAROSET.*

Both romaine lettuce and horseradish can be used for *maror.*
The horseradish—so gnarly, fleshy, and earthy—is actually a
root; it symbolizes the bitterness of slavery.

At the seder we do not eat *maror* by itself. We dip the lettuce
with the horseradish (getting a double dose of *maror*) into the
muddy-looking *charoset,* transforming the bitterness of slavery
into a surprisingly delicious treat.

Stuck in our grievances about
the past, we can be enslaved
by our own bitterness, deprived
of the fullness of our lives.

Talk about it: Consider how
you can transform your own
bitter experiences into something more palatable and even
beneficial.

RECITE TOGETHER:

בָּרוּךְ אַתָּה, יְיָ אֱלֹהֵינוּ, מֶלֶךְ הָעוֹלָם, אֲשֶׁר קִדְּשָׁנוּ
בְּמִצְוֹתָיו וְצִוָּנוּ עַל אֲכִילַת מָרוֹר.

Blessed are You, Eternal
our God, Force of the
universe, who makes us
holy with Your *mitzvot,*
by commanding us
to eat *maror.*

*Baruch Atah, Adonai
Eloheinu, Melech
ha'olam, asher
kid'shanu b'mitzvotav
v'tzivanu
al achilat maror.*

כּוֹרֵךְ
Koreich ◦ Wrapping

The word *koreich* derives from *karach*, which means "to wrap or encircle."

The Hillel Sandwich

TAKE THE BOTTOM MATZAH AND MAKE A SANDWICH OF MATZAH, *MAROR*, AND *CHAROSET*.

In ancient times, Rabbi Hillel made a wrap of the essential Passover foods. Originally matzah was soft and pliable, not hard, crunchy, and uniform like it is today. To honor Hillel, we build a Hillel sandwich: matzah topped with *maror* (either horseradish or lettuce or both) and *charoset* (no blessing needed).

The Hillel sandwich combines three essential food types: wheat, a grass that sprouts from the earth; horseradish, a root that is buried deep underground; and apples (*charoset*), a fruit that hangs from a tree.

Hillel was known for his ability to integrate conflicting truths into one whole. The Hillel sandwich blends three seder foods into one. When we unite disparate parts into one whole, we help redeem the world.

שֻׁלְחָן עוֹרֵךְ

Shulchan Oreich ∘ The Set Table

Let's eat!

צָפוּן
Tzafun ◦ Hidden

The *Afikoman*

SEARCH FOR THE *AFIKOMAN*.

Retrieving the hidden matzah is like recovering a hidden part of ourselves. At this point in the seder, matzah symbolizes our liberation. Eating it can help make us whole again.

It is fitting that the last food we partake of at the seder is matzah. We began the meal with matzah and we end with matzah. Eating matzah, we admire again the wheat and the earth from which it comes. We leave the seder with a hint of the earth in our mouths.

BREAK UP THE *AFIKOMAN* AND PASS IT AROUND. EAT THE *AFIKOMAN*.

After the meal, children search for the *afikoman*, the broken matzah. (If the children have hidden the matzah, then the adults seek.) When they find it, they bargain with the host for a reward. Offer seeds or a plant or some other simple earthy gift for the one(s) who finds the *afikoman*. Or consider making a contribution in the person's name to a conservation or environmental organization.

בָּרֵךְ
Bareich ∘ Blessing

After we've completed the meal we give thanks—not just for the food but for all the gifts we receive freely every day. Gratitude is not a passive stance. It is an act of generosity. When we offer thanks to God, we are returning to the One a measure of that which has been given to us.

POUR BUT DON'T DRINK THE THIRD CUP OF WINE. RECITE TOGETHER THE BLESSING FOR THE FOOD.

Blessed are You, Eternal our God,
Force of the universe,
Who feeds the whole world with goodness,
in grace, kindness, and compassion;
Who gives food to all the creatures; who is kind forever;
Whose great goodness ensures that we never lack for food;
Who feeds and sustains everything and does good for everything;
Who prepares food for all the creatures of creation.

בָּרוּךְ אַתָּה יְיָ, הַזָּן אֶת הַכֹּל.

Blessed are You, God,   *Baruch Atah, Adonai,*
who feeds all living things.   *hazan et hakol.*

The Talmud teaches that one who enjoys a fruit without offering a blessing is considered a thief because she robs the fruit's guardian angel of the divine energy it needs to produce another generation of fruit. (commentary on B'RACHOT 35b)

We thank You, God, Force of the universe,
for giving us a beautiful, good, and spacious land,
for taking us out of Egypt and freeing us from slavery,
for sealing Your covenant with us,
for teaching us Torah,
for granting us life, grace, and kindness,
and for the food by which You continually feed and sustain us,
every day, every season, every hour.
For it is written, "You shall eat and be satisfied, and bless the
One for the good land that is being given to you." (Deut. 8:10)

We offer thanks not just for the food (*hazan et hakol*) but also for "the land and the food" (*al ha'aretz v'al hamazon*).

בָּרוּךְ אַתָּה יְיָ, עַל הָאָרֶץ וְעַל הַמָּזוֹן.

Blessed are You, God, for the land and for the food.

Baruch Atah, Adonai, al ha'aretz v'al hamazon.

The third cup is associated with the biblical phrase "God redeemed us." (EXOD. 6:6) Freedom has always been our birthright. God redeemed us, restoring our freedom to us.

כּוֹס שְׁלִישִׁי • The Third Cup

We conclude the blessings after the meal by drinking the third cup of wine.

The third cup is dedicated to the air. This cup calls to mind *ruach Elohim*, the wind of God, hovering over creation, and the breath of life that God breathed into Adam's nostrils. It is a poignant reminder of the continuity of our breath, the air, and the weather.

בָּרוּךְ אַתָּה, יְיָ אֱלֹהֵינוּ, מֶלֶךְ הָעוֹלָם, בּוֹרֵא פְּרִי הַגָּפֶן.

Blessed are You, Eternal our God, Force of the universe, Creator of the fruit of the vine.

Baruch Atah, Adonai Eloheinu, Melech ha'olam, borei p'ri hagafen.

כּוֹס שֶׁל אֵלִיָּהוּ • Elijah's Cup

An empty cup honoring the prophet Elijah sits on the table. Elijah is known as the bearer of good news; he symbolizes hope for the future.

ASK A CHILD TO OPEN THE DOOR SO ELIJAH MAY ENTER.

Take a moment to consider your hopes and dreams. Together, we fill Elijah's cup, to show that when we all work together, we can create a better world.

Talk about it: Has anything at the seder touched you? How can you integrate what you have experienced into your life?

PASS ELIJAH'S CUP AROUND THE TABLE AND INVITE EVERYONE TO POUR SOME WINE OR JUICE FROM THEIR CUP INTO ELIJAH'S AND—IF THEY DESIRE—TO EXPRESS THEIR DREAMS FOR THE FUTURE.

RECITE TOGETHER:

May the Merciful One send Elijah the prophet to bring good news and comfort, as it says, "I send you the prophet Elijah... he will turn the hearts of the parents to their children, and the hearts of the children to their parents." (Malachi 3:23–24)

The verse bids us to listen to one another across the generational divide. Alienation between generations can lead to serious consequences for our families and for the land.

SING:

אֵלִיָּהוּ הַנָּבִיא, אֵלִיָּהוּ הַתִּשְׁבִּי,
אֵלִיָּהוּ הַגִּלְעָדִי.
בִּמְהֵרָה בְיָמֵינוּ, יָבֹא אֵלֵינוּ,
עִם מָשִׁיחַ בֶּן דָּוִד.

*Eliyahu hanavi, Eliyahu haTishbi,
Eliyahu haGiladi.
Bimheirah v'yameinu, yavo eileinu,
im Mashiach ben David.*

May Elijah the prophet, Elijah the Tishbite, Elijah of Gilead, come quickly to bring redemption.

כּוֹס שֶׁל מִרְיָם ∘ Miriam's Cup

An empty cup symbolizing Miriam's well sits on the table. Legend tells that a magical spring of healing water known as Miriam's well accompanied the Israelites through the desert for forty years. While Elijah's cup is a symbol of future times, Miriam's cup is a symbol of all that sustains us in this very moment.

Miriam's cup is also a reminder of a whole generation of women —Miriam, the midwives, Pharaoh's daughter—who maintained their faith, supported their communities, and continued to bear children against all odds. The Talmud says, "If it were not for the righteous women of that generation, we would not have been redeemed from Egypt." (*Sotah* 11b)

Together we fill Miriam's cup to remember that we are sustained by water, by women, and by our communities and our faith.

PASS MIRIAM'S CUP AROUND THE TABLE AND INVITE EVERYONE TO POUR SOME WATER FROM THEIR CUP INTO MIRIAM'S AND— IF THEY DESIRE—TO EXPRESS THEIR WISHES FOR THEMSELVES, THEIR COMMUNITIES, AND THE EARTH RIGHT NOW.

SING (TO THE TUNE OF ELIYAHU HANAVI):

Miriam han'vi'ah oz v'zimrah b'yadah
Miriam tirkod itanu l'hagdil zimrat olam.
Miriam tirkod itanu l'takein et ha'olam.
Bimheirah v'yameinu hi t'vi'einu el mei ha-y'shuah;
el mei ha'y'shuah!

Talk about it: What does *tikun olam* (Hebrew for "repairing the world") mean to you today in an era of climate change?

Miriam the prophet, strength and song in her hand,
Miriam, dance with us to increase the world's song.
Miriam, dance with us to repair the world.
Soon may she bring us to the waters of redemption.
(Rabbi Leila Gal Berner)

הַלֵּל
Hallel ∘ Praising

Hallel is Judaism's deepest gratitude practice. Reciting more psalms may seem repetitious, but the more we practice gratitude, the more grateful and joyful we'll become.

FILL THE FOURTH CUP AND PLACE IT BEFORE YOU AS YOU RECITE THE FOLLOWING PSALM OR VOICE YOUR OWN EXPRESSION OF GRATITUDE.

Give thanks to the One because God is good,
God's kindness is forever. . .
From the narrow place, I cried out to the One.
The One responded to me in a wide-open place.

What can man do to me?
God is my help. . . .

It's better to take refuge in the One than to trust in people.
It's better to take refuge in the One than to trust in princes.
All the nations surrounded me;

In the name of the One, I cut them down.
They swarmed round me, encircled me;

In the name of the One, I cut them down.
They swarmed round me like bees; . . .

In the name of the One, I cut them down. . . .

God is my strength and my song;
This for me is freedom. . . .

Open for me the gates of justice
I will enter and give thanks to the One!

This is the gateway of the One; the just will enter it.

I thank You because You answered me,
You are my freedom.
The stone the builders rejected has become the foundation stone! . . .

Give thanks to the One because God is good,
God's kindness is forever.

(Psalm 118, selected verses)

Talk about it: Consider what you are grateful for: What part of your body or what body function? Or what kind of trees? What plants? What people? What animals? What insects? What places? What waterway? What weather? What music? What books? What aspect of Judaism? What, right here in this moment?

SING:
Min hameitzar, karati Yah, anani, vamerchav Yah.

This verse associates slavery with the "narrow place," and God with a sense of spaciousness.

Singing and dancing are wonderful expressions of praise. Feel free to get up from the table to sing and stretch and dance.

SING:
Ozi v'zimrat Yah;
Vay'hi li lishuah

Talk about it: What does "God is my song" mean to you?

This psalm understands God in terms of kindness, spaciousness, help, strength, song, freedom, and goodness.

הוֹדוּ לַייָ כִּי טוֹב,
כִּי לְעוֹלָם חַסְדּוֹ....
מִן הַמֵּצַר קָרָאתִי יָּהּ,
עָנָנִי בַמֶּרְחָב יָהּ.

יְיָ לִי לֹא אִירָא, מַה יַּעֲשֶׂה לִי אָדָם.
יְיָ לִי בְּעֹזְרָי....

טוֹב לַחֲסוֹת בַּייָ מִבְּטֹחַ בָּאָדָם.
טוֹב לַחֲסוֹת בַּייָ מִבְּטֹחַ בִּנְדִיבִים.
כָּל גּוֹיִם סְבָבוּנִי בְּשֵׁם יְיָ כִּי אֲמִילַם.

סַבּוּנִי גַם סְבָבוּנִי בְּשֵׁם יְיָ כִּי אֲמִילַם.
סַבּוּנִי כִדְבֹרִים....

בְּשֵׁם יְיָ כִּי אֲמִילַם....

עָזִּי וְזִמְרָת יָהּ,
וַיְהִי לִי לִישׁוּעָה....

פִּתְחוּ לִי שַׁעֲרֵי צֶדֶק,
אָבֹא בָם אוֹדֶה יָהּ. זֶה הַשַּׁעַר לַייָ,
צַדִּיקִים יָבֹאוּ בוֹ.

אוֹדְךָ כִּי עֲנִיתָנִי,
וַתְּהִי לִי לִישׁוּעָה.
אֶבֶן מָאֲסוּ הַבּוֹנִים, הָיְתָה
לְרֹאשׁ פִּנָּה....

הוֹדוּ לַייָ כִּי טוֹב, כִּי לְעוֹלָם חַסְדּוֹ.

In reaching to find words to sing God's praise, the poet points to the fullness of the seas below and the infinite expanse of the heavens above—to the eagles soaring in the air and the gazelles loping on earth. To experience the depth of gratitude, we are given a vision of the rapture of creation.

The fourth cup is associated with the biblical phrase "I will take you to be My people and I will be your God." (EXOD. 6:7) The ultimate relationship between God and people is deeply intimate, like a marriage.

The fourth cup is dedicated to fire. Fire is the energy of the world and also the destroyer. Fire calls to mind the burning bush, the lightning at Mount Sinai, and the chariot of God. Fire is the element of the sun—of light—calling all things to emerge.

נִשְׁמַת כָּל חַי ◦ The Breath of Life Praises You

RECITE TOGETHER:

נִשְׁמַת כָּל חַי תְּבָרֵךְ אֶת שִׁמְךָ יְיָ אֱלֹהֵינוּ.

The breath of every living being shall bless Your name, God!
To You alone, we give thanks.
Even if our mouths were as full of song as the sea,
and our tongues as full of gladness as its waves,
if our lips were full of praise like the spacious heavens,
and our eyes shone like the sun and moon,
our hands outstretched like eagles' wings,
and our legs swift like gazelles,
we could still not thank you enough
for even one of the thousand thousands, thousands of thousands,
and myriad myriads of goodness
that you have bestowed upon our ancestors and upon us.

כּוֹס רְבִיעִי ◦ The Fourth Cup

The fourth cup concludes the seder.

RAISE THE FOURTH CUP, RECITE THE BLESSING TOGETHER; THEN DRINK WHILE LEANING TO THE LEFT.

בָּרוּךְ אַתָּה, יְיָ אֱלֹהֵינוּ, מֶלֶךְ הָעוֹלָם, בּוֹרֵא פְּרִי הַגָּפֶן.

Blessed are You, Eternal our God, Force of the universe, Creator of the fruit of the vine.

Baruch Atah, Adonai Eloheinu, Melech ha'olam, borei p'ri hagafen.

RECITE TOGETHER AFTER DRINKING THE WINE OR JUICE:

בָּרוּךְ אַתָּה יְיָ אֱלֹהֵינוּ מֶלֶךְ הָעוֹלָם עַל הַגֶּפֶן וְעַל פְּרִי הַגָּפֶן,
וְעַל תְּנוּבַת הַשָּׂדֶה, וְעַל אֶרֶץ חֶמְדָּה טוֹבָה וּרְחָבָה.

Blessed are You, Eternal our God, Force of the universe,
for the vine and for the fruit of the vine, and for the earth's
bounty, and for the beautiful, good, and spacious land.

נִרְצָה
Nirtzah ∘ Parting

We close with the ritual pronouncement "Next year in Jerusalem." In a wordplay on "Jerusalem," some rabbis suggested that *yeru* refers to awe, while *shalem*, like *shalom*, refers to wholeness and peace.

We pray that Jerusalem—the spiritual center for three great traditions—experience the peace that its name promises.

We pray that all people everywhere stand in awe of the heavens and the earth and know the peace that comes from living lives of wonder.

In the year to come, let us dedicate ourselves to making our cities wholesome cities, cities of peace.

This statement "Next year in Jerusalem" can be understood as a general affirmation of hope and peace for the whole world.

And let us say:

לְשָׁנָה הַבָּאָה בִּירוּשָׁלָיִם.

Lashanah haba'ah biy'rushalayim!

Next year in Jerusalem!

Next year in awe and peace!

Songs

ADIR HU ° MAJESTIC IS GOD

Adir hu, adir hu

Chorus:
*Yivneh veito b'karov, bimheirah, bimheirah,
B'yameinu b'karov. El b'neih, El b'neih
B'neih veitcha b'karov.*

Bachur hu, gadol hu, dagul hu. (chorus)

Hadur hu, vatik hu, zakai hu. (chorus)

Chasid hu, tahor hu, yachid hu. (chorus)

Kabir hu, lamud hu, melech hu. (chorus)

Nora hu, sagiv hu, izuz hu. (chorus)

Podeh hu, tzadik hu, kadosh hu. (chorus)

Rachum hu, shaddai hu, takif hu. (chorus)

Majestic is God, majestic is God

Chorus:
May God build God's house soon,
Speedily in our time, soon. God, build it; God, build it,
Build Your house soon!

Supreme is God, great is God, outstanding is God. (chorus)

Glorious is God, faithful is God, worthy is God. (chorus)

Kind is God, pure is God, unique is God. (chorus)

Mighty is God, wise is God, majestic is God. (chorus)

Awesome is God, strong is God, powerful is God. (chorus)

Redeeming is God, righteous is God, holy is Gdo. (chorus)

Compassionate is God, almighty is God, resolute is God.
(chorus)

This poem was written in Germany in the fifteenth century and recounts the divine attributes of God in alphabetical order.

ORAH HI ° SHE IS LIGHT

A feminist version of Adir Hu

Orah hi, orah hi

Chorus:
*Tivneh veitah b'karov, bimheirah, bimheirah, b'yameinu b'karov,
elah b'ni, elah b'ni, b'ni veiteich b'karov.*

Binah hi, gilah hi, dim'ah hi. (chorus)

Hadar hi, vered hi, zerem hi. (chorus)

Chiddush hi, tabur hi, yichud hi. (chorus)

Keseh hi, leidah hi, ma'yan hi. (chorus)

Nechamah hi, selichah hi, otzmah hi. (chorus)

Pidyon hi, tzedek hi, kodesh hi. (chorus)

Ra'ya hi, shonah hi, tamah hi. (chorus)

She is light, she is light

Chorus:
May She build Her house speedily and in our days.
God, build Your house soon—close to us in time and space.

She is wisdom, She is joy, She is tears. (chorus)

She is splendor, She is a rose, She is a flowing stream. (chorus)

She is renewal, She is the center, She is oneness. (chorus)

She is the full moon, She is birth, She is the fountain-source. (chorus)

She is comfort, She is forgiveness, She is strength. (chorus)

She is redemption, She is righteousness, She is holiness. (chorus)

She is a friend, She is changing, She is complete. (chorus)

—Rabbi Jill Hammer

67

ECHAD MI YODEI'A? ∘ WHO KNOWS ONE?

Echad mi yodei'a? Echad ani yodei'a:
Echad Eloheinu shebashamayim uva'aretz.

Sh'nayim mi yodei'a? Sh'nayim ani yodei'a: Sh'nei luchot
habrit, echad Eloheinu shebashamayim uva'aretz.

Sh'loshah mi yodei'a? Sh'loshah ani yodei'a: Sh'loshah avot,
sh'nei luchot habrit, echad Eloheinu shebashamayim uva'aretz.

(continue as above)

Arba mi yodei'a? Arba ani yodei'a: Arba imahot . . .

Chamishah mi yodei'a? Chamishah ani yodei'a: Chamishah
chumshei Torah . . .

Shishah mi yodei'a? Shishah ani yodei'a: Shishah sidrei Mishnah . . .

Shivah mi yodei'a? Shivah ani yodei'a: Shivah y'mei shabata . . .

Sh'monah mi yodei'a? Sh'monah ani yodei'a: Sh'monah
y'mei milah . . .

Tishah mi yodei'a? Tishah ani yodei'a: Tishah yarchei leidah . . .

Asarah mi yodei'a? Asarah ani yodei'a: Asarah dibraya . . .

Achad asar mi yodei'a? Achad asar ani yodei'a: Achad asar kochvaya . . .

Sh'neim asar mi yodei'a? Sh'neim asar ani yodei'a: Sh'neim asar shivtaya . . .

Sh'loshah asar mi yodei'a? Sh'loshah asar ani yodei'a: Sh'loshah
asar midaya . . .

"Echad Mi Yodei'a" is based on a German folk song from the fifteenth century. It functions like a Jewish trivia game.

Who knows one? I know one.
One is our God in heaven and on earth.

Who knows two? I know two. Two are the tablets of the
Covenant. One is our God in heaven and on earth.

Who knows three? I know three. Three are the patriarchs.
Two are the tablets of the Covenant. One is our God in heaven
and on earth.

(continue as above)

Four are the matriarchs.

Five are the books of the Torah.

Six are the sections of the Mishnah.

Seven are the days of the week.

Eight are the days to circumcision.

Nine are the months to childbirth.

Ten are the Commandments.

Eleven are the stars in Joseph's dream.

Twelve are the tribes of Israel.

Thirteen are the attributes of God.

68

This song can be sung to the traditional melody for "Echad Mi Yodei'a?" You can sing it with the Hebrew opening or start right off with the English.

ORGANIC "WHO KNOWS ONE?"

Echad mi yodei'a? Echad ani yodei'a!
One! Who knows one? One! I know one.
One is the unity, the unity, the unity, the unity,
the unity of all that is.

Sh'nayim mi yodei'a? Sh'nayim ani yodei'a!
Two! Who knows two? Two! I know two.
Two is a cell that divides to make life.

Sh'loshah mi yodei'a? Sh'loshah ani yodei'a!
Three! Who knows three? Three! I know three.
Three is the truth that reconciles duality.

Arba mi yodei'a? Arba ani yodei'a!
Four! Who knows four? Four! I know four.
Four are the elements: earth, air, water, fire.

Chamishah mi yodei'a? Chamishah ani yodei'a!
Five! Who knows five? Five! I know five.
Five is the rose that delights the eye.

Shishah mi yodei'a? Shishah ani yodei'a!
Six! Who knows six? Six! I know six.
Six is the snowflake falling from the sky.

Shivah mi yodei'a? Shivah ani yodei'a!
Seven! Who knows seven? Seven! I know seven.
Seven is the Sabbath, Creation's day.

Sh'monah mi yodei'a? Sh'monah ani yodei'a!
Eight! Who knows eight? Eight! I know eight.
Eight on its side is infinity.

Tishah mi yodei'a? Tishah ani yodei'a!
Nine! Who knows nine? Nine! I know nine.
Nine are the moons of pregnancy.

Asarah mi yodei'a? Asarah ani yodei'a!
Ten! Who knows ten? Ten! I know ten.
Ten are the laws that sustain society.

Achad asar mi yodei'a? Achad asar ani yodei'a!
Eleven! Who knows eleven? Eleven! I know eleven.
Eleven are the stars in Joseph's dream.

Sh'neim asar mi yodei'a? Sh'neim asar ani yodei'a!
Twelve! Who knows twelve? Twelve! I know twelve.
Twelve are the signs of each person's birth.

Sh'loshah asar mi yodei'a? Sh'loshah asar ani yodei'a!
Thirteen! Who knows thirteen? Thirteen! I know thirteen.
Thirteen times the moon turns round the earth.

—Rabba Kaya Stern-Kaufman

CHAD GADYA

Chad gadya, chad gadya, dizvan aba bitrei zuzei,
chad gadya, chad gadya.

Vaata shunra, v'achlah l'gadya, dizvan aba bitrei zuzei,
chad gadya, chad gadya.

Vaata chalba, v'nashach l'shunra, d'achlah l'gadya,
dizvan aba bitrei zuzei, chad gadya, chad gadya.

Vaata chutra, v'hikah l'chalba, d'nashach l'shunra, d'achlah l'gadya,
dizvan aba bitrei zuzei, chad gadya, chad gadya.

Vaata nura, v'saraf l'chutra, d'hikah l'chalba,
d'nashach l'shunra, d'achlah l'gadya, dizvan aba bitrei zuzei,
chad gadya, chad gadya.

Vaata maya, v'chavah l'nura, d'saraf l'chutra, d'hikah l'chalba,
d'nashach l'shunra, d'achlah l'gadya, dizvan aba bitrei zuzei,
chad gadya, chad gadya.

Vaata tora, v'shatah l'maya, d'chavah l'nura, d'saraf l'chutra,
d'hikah l'chalba, d'nashach l'shunra, d'achlah l'gadya, dizvan aba
bitrei zuzei, chad gadya, chad gadya.

Vaata hashocheit, v'shachat l'tora, d'shatah l'maya, d'chavah l'nura,
d'saraf l'chutra, d'hikah l'chalba, d'nashach l'shunra, d'achlah
l'gadya, dizvan aba bitrei zuzei, chad gadya, chad gadya.

Vaata mal'ach hamavet, v'shachat l'shocheit, d'shachat l'tora,
d'shatah l'maya, d'chavah l'nura, d'saraf l'chutra, d'hikah l'chalba,
d'nashach l'shunra, d'achlah l'gadya, dizvan aba bitrei zuzei,
chad gadya, chad gadya.

Vaata Hakadosh Baruch Hu, v'shachat l'mal'ach hamavet, d'shachat
l'shocheit, d'shachat l'tora, d'shatah l'maya, d'chavah l'nura, d'saraf
l'chutra, d'hikah l'chalba, d'nashach l'shunra, d'achlah l'gadya,
dizvan aba bitrei zuzei, chad gadya, chad gadya.

"Chad Gadya" is based on a German nursery rhyme that derives from an old French nursery rhyme. Some commentators imagined it as a capsule of Jewish history in which one oppressor, symbolized by an animal, always comes along to swallow another, until God arrives to redeem the world. In ecological terms, one can imagine an ecosystem in which we are all subject to the vagaries of weather (water and fire in the song) and the natural processes of predator-prey relationships.

One little goat, one little goat, my father bought for
two *zuzim, chad gadya, chad gadya.*

Then came the cat that ate the goat my father bought for two *zuzim,
chad gadya, chad gadya.*

Then came the dog that bit the cat that ate the goat my father
bought for two *zuzim, chad gadya, chad gadya.*

(continue as above)

Then came the stick that beat the dog . . .

Then came the fire that burned the stick . . .

Then came the water that quenched the fire . . .

Then came the ox that drank the water . . .

Then came the butcher that killed the ox . . .

Then came the angel of death that slew the butcher . . .

(final verse)

Then came the Holy One that destroyed the angel of death
that slew the butcher that killed the ox that drank the water
that quenched the fire that burned the stick that beat the dog
that bit the cat that ate the goat my father bought for two *zuzim,
chad gadya, chad gadya.*

Counting the Omer

The forty-nine-day period between the second night of Passover and Shavuot is called the omer. In ancient times, the omer period marked the completion of the growing cycle of the grains. Barley and wheat were sown in the fall on Sukkot. Barley would begin to fruit at Passover, and it was offered at the Temple in gratitude from Passover until Shavuot. By Shavuot, the wheat, which takes longer to ripen, would be ready, and it would be offered up to God in the form of bread.

Originally, the omer period was a season of high anxiety. While Israel's primary food crops—olives, grapes, and pomegranates —needed successive days of heat to bloom, wheat and barley needed cool air. If the dry, hot *chamsin* winds came too soon, the entire grain crop could be destroyed. On the other hand, while the wheat needed rains in its final stages of the ripening, the same rain could devastate the fruit crop. During the omer, the Israelites would carefully attend to the weather and their crops.

"On the strength of counting the omer, Abraham, our father, inherited the land."
—LEVITICUS RABBAH

"If we have no flour, we have no Torah."—PIRKEI AVOT 3:21

Omer means "sheaf" (of grain), and it is also a unit of measurement.

Today the counting of the omer can be a mindfulness exercise. Counting each day reminds us of the preciousness of our weather and our crops. We count beginning the second night of Passover.

STAND AND RECITE THE BLESSING; THEN RECITE THE APPROPRIATE DAY OF THE COUNT.

בָּרוּךְ אַתָּה, יְיָ אֱלֹהֵינוּ, מֶלֶךְ הָעוֹלָם, אֲשֶׁר קִדְּשָׁנוּ בְּמִצְוֹתָיו וְצִוָּנוּ עַל סְפִירַת הָעֹמֶר.

Blessed are You, Eternal our God, Force of the universe, who makes us holy with Your *mitzvot,* by commanding us to count the omer.

Baruch Atah, Adonai Eloheinu, Melech ha'olam, asher kid'shanu b'mitzvotav v'tzivanu al s'phirat ha'omer.

הַיּוֹם יוֹם אֶחָד לָעֹמֶר.

Hayom yom echad la'omer.

Today is the first day of the omer.

Author's Note:
The Promise of the Land

The Ecological Meaning of Land

When Behrman House contacted me about writing an ecologically focused haggadah, I wasn't sure I was the right person for the job. I had always enjoyed the animated seder table conversations in my communities. I connected to my ancient ancestors and the wilderness by eating matzah, horseradish, and *charoset,* and by taking desert treks during the week of Passover. I could sense in my bones the freedom that spring brings after a long, hard winter. But try as I might, I had never experienced what the haggadah asks of us—to feel as if we were slaves liberated by a magisterial God. The central section of the haggadah, the *maggid*, the story of Passover, left me cold. If I were to write a kind of "green" haggadah, I would need to find some ecological perspective grounding our grand narrative.

I had already been on a lifelong journey exploring the ecological roots of Judaism. In the early days of the Jewish environmental movement, many of us scoured the (Hebrew) Bible and other Jewish texts, identifying particular verses or ideas as ecological. But a collection of verses does not constitute a worldview. I always intuited that there must be something more. That the ancient Israelites had spent forty years (and most of the Torah) trekking across a desert wilderness, living in tents, encountering God on mountaintops and by rivers, spoke to me of a way of life that was inextricably bound to the natural world and the land.

I realized I needed to take the idea of "land" more seriously. After all, it was the land—mountains, river valleys, forests—that moved me. Ecologically speaking, land is a fundamental concept. Land is the community to which we belong. It is our habitat and we are its inhabitants. It is an interdependent ecosystem of soils, waters, plants, and animals. Farmers have always known the value of land. Agrarian author Wendell Berry famously wrote, "If you have no land you have nothing: no food, no shelter, no warmth, no freedom, no life."

Still it can be hard for some to imagine that something so lowly, so inconspicuous and ordinary as land or soil, could have much value. Many people associate land and soil with dirt—something to rid ourselves of—never recognizing it as the ground of our being. On the other hand, many associate the word "land"—in a Jewish context—with the land of Israel only and are unable to recognize *the* land more universally as *any* land, as earth. As physicists have taught us, if you focus on a particle, it's impossible to see the wave.

The Promise of Land in the Torah

Curious about land's place in the Bible, I ran a quick word search and was surprised to find that the word "land" itself (actually two words, *adamah* and *eretz*) appears more than two thousand five hundred times. Perhaps the ubiquity of land in our text prevents us from actually seeing it—the same way that we easily lose sight of the ground or land upon which we walk.

With more study, I began to understand the whole Torah, starting with the Garden of Eden, as the story of a people and a land. In the beginning we Israelites were landless. Then God made a promise to Abraham and to Isaac after him and to Jacob and all the subsequent generations that we would inherit a land that we could call home.

En route to the promised land, we would endure four hundred years in Egypt, where Pharaoh owned and exploited the land and everyone in it. For Pharaoh, land had no inherent value; it was a commodity. Utilizing slave labor, Pharaoh increased the land's agricultural output, amassing more and more wealth for the royal coffers.

Living so long in Pharaoh's exploitive economy, we would come to forget the meaning of land. If God were to give us a land, we would need to recognize the land's incomparable value. God took us to the wilderness for forty years to teach us that land, the earth, was not a "thing"; it was not ours to acquire, and it was not guaranteed. Land, people, and God were imperceptibly bound in a three-way covenant relationship—knit together as one.

The Promise of Land in the Haggadah

What does all this have to do with our haggadah, the story of Passover?

When the instructions for what would become the seder were written down in the second century CE, the rabbis stipulated that—along with drinking four cups of wine, asking three questions (originally there were three, not four), discussing *pesach*, matzah, and *maror*, and reciting psalms and blessings—we were charged to read one biblical passage in its entirety. That passage encapsulates the Jewish story and can be summed up like this:

> My father was a wandering Aramean.
>
> We went down to Egypt and multiplied there.
>
> The Egyptians imposed harsh labor on us and oppressed us.
>
> We cried out to God and God heard our voice.
>
> God led us out of Egypt with signs and wonders.
>
> **And God gave us a land.**
>
> **And now we bring the first fruits of the land, which You, God, have given to us.** (Deut. 26:5–10)

But by the time the actual haggadah was composed several centuries later, the last two verses (in bold above) had been dropped.

What is the nature of these two verses? And why were they dropped from the haggadah?

1. "And God gave us a land" (Deut. 26:9): The days of slavery, oppression, and wandering were over. Now we would have a land to inhabit and care for—a land in which to grow our food and pasture our animals, build our shelters, and live our lives. Land meant freedom. There is nothing more valuable than land.

2. "And now we bring the first fruits of the land, which You, God, have given to us" (Deut. 26:10): Each spring when the fruits were finally ripe on the vine, we would set aside the first, most perfect ones for God. That which was most precious to us, we would bring to God as an expression of our gratitude for the land and our recognition that God—not us—is the owner of all land and everything in it. In the words of the psalmist, "The earth is Adonai's and all of its fullness." (Ps. 24:1) In returning the fruits to God, we were participating in the eternal round of giving and receiving.

The Ecological Message of the Haggadah

While the rabbis didn't explain why they deleted these two verses from the haggadah, we can infer a possibility. The very first instructions for the seder—including the two verses—were probably written a generation or two after the destruction of the Second Temple in Jerusalem (70 CE), when—even though many Jews had scattered to other lands—there was still a sizable Jewish population in Israel. These two verses assume the Israelites were living in the land of Israel and offering the fruits of that land in the Temple in Jerusalem.

But by the end of the Bar Kochba Rebellion in 135 CE and the Roman occupation of Jerusalem, many more Jews were living in exile and had no land to which they belonged. By the third century, these verses may have been omitted because the reality of life in exile was so far from the vision of what the Jews thought they had been promised—a land where they could dwell in peace and safety.

Yet without these two verses, it's easy to forget why God chose to free us from slavery in the first place. God led us out of Egypt because God had promised us a land, so that we could live as a free people. But we would only inherit the land if we honored our covenantal relationship by living good, wholesome, and righteous lives. If we behaved unethically or irresponsibly toward each other, the land, or God, we could lose the land.

Without these two verses, it's also easy to conceive of God as a triumphal deity and the Israelites as the passive recipients of God's largesse. These two verses portray God as a partner in a dynamic reciprocal relationship with a people who are actors in their own destiny.

I realized that by retrieving these two verses and returning them back to the central Jewish narrative, the Passover haggadah could convey a profound ecological message. I offer them to you here with the hope that this seder can remind us of our deep ecological heritage, inspire us to rejoice in the fullness of the earth, and lead us to live lives that honor Hamakom, the One whose presence fills every place.

Preparing for the Seder

Creating a Beautiful and Ecological Seder

Too often we subscribe to the idea that more is better—that a more lavish Passover meal is preferable. Yet, a simple and elegant meal can be extremely satisfying. Remember that the seder commemorates a trek in the desert, where our ancestors would have enjoyed the most basic foods. At its root, Passover is an homage to simplicity.

Since your guests will be eating plenty of appetizers for the *karpas* step in the seder—including green vegetables, potatoes, and dips—they may welcome a less elaborate yet tasty meal. There's something pleasurable about eating just enough to satisfy your hunger. Consuming sensibly at the seder can help us get in the habit of consuming sensibly in the rest of our lives.

For your main course, consider a vegetarian meal, or include a vegetarian or vegan option in addition to a traditional meat, fish, or poultry dish. Vegetarian dishes require fewer resources and take less energy to produce. Guests with food allergies or special diets often prefer vegetarian or vegan offerings and will be appreciative of your efforts to include them.

The atmosphere of the room will add as much to feeling full and fulfilled as the food you eat. Consider everything that will contribute to the beauty of the seder—the physical space, the fragrances, the colors, shapes, and tastes of the foods; the conversation. Some of us may assume that we need a white tablecloth, matching napkins, and a coordinated set of dishes for a proper seder. Happily, these days, such conventional ideas about elegance no longer dictate what our seders look like. Think eclectic; think individuality; think freedom. So bring out the fabrics and dishes that you love. Your seder will be much more earth-friendly if you set your table with reusable cloths and dinnerware.

Adorning your home with early spring flowers, like daffodils or forsythia, or any green growing things will add to the beauty of the celebration and will remind your guests that Passover heralds the coming of spring. If you have your own garden, pick whatever is in bloom. Consider dressing up your table with the leafy greens that can be used for *karpas*, the appetizer you will be eating at the seder. In some Sephardic traditions, Jews adorn the table itself with all the ritual foods of the seder, forgoing the seder plate altogether.

Passover affords us abundant opportunities to adopt healthy habits for ourselves and for the earth. It's an ideal time of year to commit to new life-affirming and sustainable practices.

Conscious Purchasing

"There is a Chasidic custom to avoid any processed food on Passover, in order to stay clear of the accidental consumption of *chameitz*. Imagine an entire meal prepared without plastic packaging, machine manipulation, or unknown ingredients. Imagine how that food—just one step removed from the land—can help us to feel connected to the source of life."
—JONATHAN DUBINSKY

Purchase fresh, locally grown products without preservatives or packaging. You can also find a variety of artisanal kosher-for-Passover items. These days, some young Jews, in an effort to live more simply and closer to the land, have turned to farming, and some are preparing products that are kosher for Passover. By purchasing these products, you are supporting the people who grow your foods and the healthy treatment of the land.

As you prepare for the seder, you may want to think about a prize for the winner of the *afikoman* hunt. Consider a plant, gardening supplies, or other earth-friendly gift. Or perhaps you want to make a donation to a favorite environmental or conservation organization in the winner's name.

Conscious purchasing also means limiting waste. Bring reusable bags to the store, including smaller bags for produce and nuts. If it's necessary to purchase paper goods, biodegradable paper products are best. Look for unbleached and recycled products, ideally with 100 percent post-consumer content. If you must use disposable utensils and cups, try to find bioplastics. It's best to stay away from Styrofoam and disposable plastic utensils, plastic packaging, plastic table coverings, and composites like hot cups or poly-lined plates.

You can also reduce waste when cleaning up after the seder. Save old containers to use for leftovers, and encourage guests to bring containers so that they can take home leftovers, too. Try to divert as much waste as possible from landfills and incinerators. Establish a spot in your kitchen where you can set up three bins, each with its own sign: Compost (if you have a compost pile), Recycling, and Trash.

"When we host large gatherings, there's often a temptation to grab the disposable plates and cutlery so that we can maximize time with the guests and minimize time in the kitchen. However, remember:

1) Passover is special! Elevate the mood of the seder with china, not Chinet.

2) Create community by asking for help. We often avoid asking guests to help clean up, imagining they will interpret clean-up as a chore. But guests often appreciate being asked to help. This can create a wonderful opportunity to wind down while participating in a mutually beneficial project."
—JONATHAN DUBINSKY

The Symbolic Foods of the Seder

Matzah (symbolizing affliction and liberation): Making matzah is a great way to connect to the elemental aspects of the holiday. While it's complicated to make matzah at home, since it is difficult to ensure that matzah is kosher for Passover, you may find opportunities to bake matzah in synagogue kitchens. Or you can purchase handmade round *sh'murah* matzah (matzah that is "watched" from harvesting until it's packaged) from specialty stores or online, or you can ask your grocer to order it. Each handmade matzah with its burnt edges and wavy texture adds character to the seder table. Of course, you can also purchase regular matzah at the grocery store.

Wine (symbolizing joy and transformation): Many years ago sweet Manischewitz was the only kosher-for-Passover wine available, but today we have many options. Consider assigning the job of selecting wines to one of your wine-loving guests. Remember to provide grape juice for children and for those who prefer it.

Some people serve hard-boiled eggs with their *karpas* course. Eggs symbolize the roundness of life and the renewal of spring, and they keep guests satisfied as they engage in lively Passover conversations before the formal meal.

Karpas (a green vegetable symbolizing spring): People commonly use parsley for *karpas*. Yet here too, there are many choices. *Karpas* refers to a green vegetable arising from the earth; you can experiment with various greens. In many places, the first vegetable to sprout up is asparagus, so it's fitting to use it for *karpas*. Asparagus can connect you to the earth, and because it's fleshy rather than leafy, it can help stave off hunger. Consider including lots of greens for *karpas*, like cilantro, arugula, and watercress—they all taste earthy and signify spring. Use what is local and tasty to you.

Generations back, Ashkenazi Jews in eastern Europe used potatoes for *karpas* because it was impossible to find fresh green vegetables in April. Today, in honor of this tradition, many people still enjoy potatoes for *karpas*. Potatoes (boiled, roasted, or baked) are dense and hearty, making them a filling snack that can be eaten throughout the seder.

Zeroa (a roasted shank bone symbolizing God's outstretched arm): The shank bone recalls the Passover sacrifice and ancient Israel's pastoral culture. You may be able to get one from your grocer. If your guests are vegetarians, then a roasted beet is a popular substitute.

Beitzah (burnt egg symbolizing the festival offering): You may be able to purchase eggs from local farmers or—if you're lucky—from friends who raise chickens in their backyards. If you buy from a grocery store, look for free-range or cage-free eggs. The chickens who laid these eggs run about freely and live healthier lives than industrially farmed ones.

Maror (bitter herbs representing slavery): While in ancient times a type of bitter lettuce was used for *maror*, for the past nine hundred years, horseradish—even though it is a root—has been adopted as the bitter herb of choice among Ashkenazi Jews. In southern and western Europe and Mediterranean countries, lettuce and endive are still used for *maror* today. Horseradish probably became popular for the same reason that potatoes did for *karpas*—because in colder, eastern Europe, the lettuce didn't leaf out in time for Passover.

Fresh horseradish is a wonderfully curious and gnarly root that can stimulate questions and conversation. Most grocery stores carry fresh horseradish root, which can be more interesting (and ecologically sound) to use than the minced variety. You will need to grate some and apportion it in dipping bowls, so that everyone can partake of it.

Chazeret (a second bitter herb, usually romaine lettuce, also representing slavery): Two bitter herbs usually sit on the seder plate: *maror*, typically horseradish, and *chazeret*, or lettuce—although not all seder plates have a spot for *chazeret*. Both kinds of bitter herbs can be used for the *maror* blessing and the Hillel sandwich.

Charoset (fruit-nut-spice mixture representing the mortar used in constructing Pharaoh's cities): Ashkenazi Jews typically make *charoset* by dicing up apples and adding chopped walnuts, spices, and red wine. Sephardic Jews use a combination of dates, other dried fruits, bananas, oranges, pistachios, and almonds. The texture should resemble something between a fruit salad and a fruit paste. Experiment with *charoset* from other Jewish Diaspora communities, such as Greece and Yemen. *Charoset* is a crowd pleaser, so be sure to have plenty on hand.

While some claim that in ancient times the Talmud permitted beets on the seder plate as a substitute for the shank bone, it seems more likely that beets were just a popular side dish.
(commentary on P'SACHIM 114B)

Seder Checklist

You'll need to provide the following items for the seder table:

- ❏ *Haggadot*
- ❏ Pitcher of water, bowl, and towel for hand-washing
- ❏ Seder plate, with the following ritual foods:
    - ○ Roasted shank bone or beet, burned or scorched
    - ○ Parsley, cilantro, arugula, asparagus, or any green vegetable(s) for *karpas*
    - ○ Horseradish root for *maror*, the bitter herb
    - ○ Romaine lettuce for *chazeret*, the second bitter herb
    - ○ A bowl of *charoset*
    - ○ A roasted egg
- ❏ A plate with three pieces of matzah, wrapped in a special cloth
- ❏ Other ritual foods and items
    - ○ Candlesticks, candles, and matches
    - ○ Kiddush cup
    - ○ Elijah's cup, a special cup for wine
    - ○ Miriam's cup, a special cup for water
- ❏ Serving platters and bowls with extra matzah, *karpas*, grated horseradish, romaine lettuce, and *charoset*, and small bowls with salt water
- ❏ Wine or grape juice—enough for each participant to drink four cups
- ❏ Pillows for reclining (optional)

Optional: potatoes for *karpas*

Some people place an orange on the seder plate as a symbol of inclusion. Some put an olive on the plate to symbolize the hope for peace between Israelis and Palestinians; or a coffee bean to symbolize contemporary types of slavery. Feel free to add symbolic foods that have meaning to you.

Optional: hard boiled eggs for snacking

Acknowledgments

From the Author

This haggadah was a labor of love for everyone involved in its production. It was so gratifying to work with a team of people at Behrman House who were as committed to this project as I was. Thanks so much to Dena Neusner, who paid loving attention to every word and detail, and to Zahava Bogner for her brilliant design. An enormous thank you to Galia Goodman for embracing this project wholeheartedly and bringing the haggadah to life through her gorgeous artwork.

A special thanks to Steve Altarescu, Rachel Brodie, Sara Brown, Barbara Burkhart, Ted Hiebert, Gillian Kendall, Jonathan Brumberg Kraus, Laurie Levy, Mordechai Liebling, Vivie Mayer, Jonathan Rubinstein, Rami Shapiro, and Daniel Swartz for their friendship and for giving so generously of their time in providing comments on the haggadah.

Lastly, I am so amazed and grateful to be married to my treasured husband and traveling companion, Steven Tenenbaum, who continually delights me with words and music and keeps me tethered to the earth.

Ellen Bernstein
Connecticut River Watershed
Holyoke, Massachusetts

From the Artist

As a lifelong hiker, I feel a strong connection to the land in its many forms, especially the long trails here and in other countries. The art in this haggadah is the product of this connection, and of many seasons of my life and my community. I would like to thank the people, especially Steve Botnick, who agreed to have their art of mine photographed so it could be reproduced in *The Promise of the Land*. I also want to thank my Jewish community, especially my rabbis Steve Sager, Daniel Greyber, and Frank Fischer (of blessed memory), for their consistent encouragement.

My partner of over thirty years, Meredith Emmett, as well as my extended family, students, neighbors, and community, have provided generous encouragement and support throughout my career as an artist and during this project. A special thank you goes to my neighbor K Brown and his wife Dana who generously stepped in to help photograph and prepare my art for publication: you are bright and generous souls with an eye for beauty, form and composition! And finally, thank you to Ellen Bernstein, Dena Neusner, and Behrman House for taking a chance on an artist who you discovered through a Google search.

Galia Goodman
Durham, North Carolina

Contributors

I am so grateful to the following people who enriched the haggadah with their own voices:

Judy Dornstreich, co-founder and co-director, Branch Creek Farm (since 1978)

Jonathan Dubinsky, Teva Network, stay-at-home dad, sustainability engineer

Daron Joffe, biodynamic farmer; founding director, Coastal Roots Farm; author, *Citizen Farmer*

Charlie Miller, principal and founder, Roofmeadow

Nati Passow, co-founder and executive director, The Jewish Farm School

Kaya Stern-Kaufman, rabba, spiritual counselor, founder of Rimon Center for Jewish Spirituality

Ben Weiner, rabbi, Jewish Community of Amherst; homesteader

Permissions

"i thank You God for most this amazing". Copyright 1950, © 1978, 1991 by the Trustees for the E. E. Cummings Trust. Copyright © 1979 by George James Firmage, from COMPLETE POEMS: 1904-1962 by E. E. Cummings, edited by George J. Firmage. Used by permission of Liveright Publishing Corporation.

"Orah Hi" by Rabbi Jill Hammer, from the *Ma'yan Women's Haggadah*, used with permission.

"Miriam Han'vi'ah" by Rabbi Leila Gal Berner, used with permission.

"Organic 'Who Knows One?'," by Rabba Kaya Stern-Kaufman, used with permission.

Biblical Citations

The Passover story on pages 26–35 is based on the following verses from the Bible:

"My father was a wandering Aramean": Gen. 24:10; 37:3–36; 39:1–20; 41:1–49

"He went down to Egypt with few numbers and sojourned there": Gen. 41:53–46:27

"And there he became a great nation, mighty and numerous": Gen. 47:11,27; Exod. 1:7–10

"The Egyptians dealt harshly with us . . .": Exod. 1:11–19

"We cried out to Adonai, the God of our ancestors . . .": Exod. 2:23–25; 3:7–9; 6:5–6,13

"Then Adonai took us out of Egypt with a mighty hand . . .": Exod. 7–11; 14:19–29

"Adonai brought us to this place and gave us this land . . .": Num. 32:13; Ps. 24:1; Lev. 25:1–23; 19:9–10; Deut. 28:15–68

"Now, I bring the first fruits of the soil . . .": Deut. 11:14–15

Sources

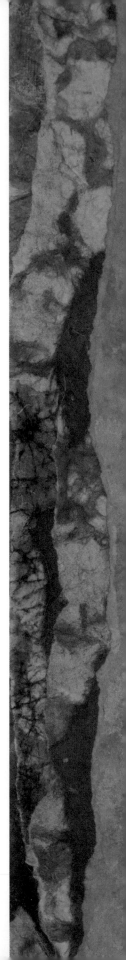

Berry, Wendell. "The Agrarian Standard." In *The Unsettling of America*. San Francisco: Sierra Club Books, 1977.

Bradford, Sarah. *Scenes in the Life of Harriet Tubman*. Auburn: W.J . Moses, 1869.

Brueggemann, Walter. *The Land*. Philadelphia: Fortress Press, 1977.

Ehrenkranz, Joel, and Deborah Sampson. "Origin of the Old Testament Plagues: Explications and Implications." *Yale Journal of Biology and Medicine* 8, no. 1 (2008): 31–42. These scholars proposed that the plagues may have resulted from an El Nino Southern oscillation.

Epstein, Marc Michael. *The Medieval Haggadah*. New Haven, CT: Yale University Press, 2011.

Garouste, Gerard, and Marc-Alain Ouaknin. *Haggadah: The Passover Story*. New York: Assouline Publishing, 2001.

Guggenheimer, Heinrich. *The Scholar's Haggadah*. Northvale, NJ: Jason Aronson, 1995.

Haggadot.com. https://www.haggadot.com.

Hirsch, Samson Raphael. *Nineteen Letters*. 1836. Sefaria. https://www.sefaria.org/Nineteen_Letters?lang=bi. In the nineteenth century, Rabbi Hirsch captured the idea that the land did not belong to us; we belonged to the land. This has become a popular idea among Jewish environmentalists.

Hoffman, Lawrence, ed. *The Land of Israel: Jewish Perspectives*. Notre Dame, IN: University of Notre Dame, 1986.

Kgositsile, W. Keorapetse. "Malcolm X and the Black Revolution." In *Malcolm X: The Man and His Times*, edited by John Henrik Clarke. Trenton, NJ: Africa World Press, 1990.

Kook, Abraham Isaac. "Passover: Who Is Free?" Adapted from *Celebration of the Soul*. Rav Kook Torah. http://www.ravkooktorah.org/PESACH60.htm.

Laufer, R. Nathan. *Leading the Passover Seder*. Woodstock, VT: Jewish Lights, 2005.

Lazarus, Emma. *An Epistle to the Hebrews*. New York: Jewish Historical Society of New York, 1883.

L'Engle, Madeleine. *A Circle of Quiet*. New York: HarperCollins, 1984.

Leopold, Aldo. *A Sand County Almanac*. Oxford: Oxford University Press, 1949.

Levinas, Emmanuel. *Nine Talmudic Readings*. Bloomington: Indiana University Press, 1990.

Marks, Gil. *Encyclopedia of Jewish Foods*. Hoboken, NJ: Wiley and Sons, 2010.

Piercy, Marge. *Pesach for the Rest of Us*. New York: Schocken Books, 2007.

Roosevelt, Franklin D. "Letter to all State Governors on a Uniform Soil Conservation Law." 1937. http://www.oxfordreference.com/view/10.1093acr ef/9780191843730.001.0001/q-oro-ed5-00008907.

Sacks, Jonathan. *The Jonathan Sacks Haggada*. Jerusalem: Koren Press Books, 2013.

The Schechter Haggadah. Jerusalem: Schechter Institute of Jewish Studies, 2007.

Silver, David. *A Passover Haggadah: Go Forth and Learn*. Philadelphia: Jewish Publication Society, 2011.

Zion, Noam, and David Dishon. *A Different Night*. Jerusalem: Shalom Hartman Institute, 1997.